Stephen Gardiner was born in London in 1925 and was educated at Dulwich College and the Architectural Association School of Architecture, where he qualified as an architect. He has taught at the Oxford School of Architecture, the Architectural Association and the Polytechnic of Central London. In 1957 he went into architectural practice and became increasingly involved as an architectural critic. From 1964–8 he worked for *London Magazine*, from 1968–70 for *The Spectator*, and since 1970 for *The Observer*. He has been a frequent broadcaster on radio and television on both architecture and the fine arts, and has contributed to various journals, including *Architectural Review* and *Sunday Times*. His publications include a thriller, *Death is an Artist* (1959), and *Evolution of the House* (1974).

Modern Masters

Le Corbusier

Stephen Gardiner

Fontana/Collins

First published in Fontana 1974
Copyright © Stephen Gardiner 1974
Printed in Great Britain
for the Publishers Wm Collins Sons & Co Ltd,
14 St James's Place, London SW1
by Richard Clay (The Chaucer Press), Ltd,
Bungay, Suffolk

Contents

Acknowledgements

All the illustrations reproduced in this book are from the collection of Lucien Hervé, Paris, except for : Redfern Gallery, 2; Editions Pierre Cailler, Geneva (*Faunes et Nymphes de Pablo Picasso*, Andre Verdet) 23; Heidi Weber, Zurich, 13, 21.

The author is grateful to the following for their assistance : Eileen Gray, Maxwell Fry, Jane Drew, Heidi Weber, Lucien Hervé, Stuart Hampshire, Denys Lasdun.

For permission to quote W. H. Auden's dedication to Christopher Isherwood from *Poems* (1930) grateful acknowledgement is due to Faber and Faber.

Illustrations

To Andrew, Becky and Hidalgo Moya

Let us honour if we can
The vertical man
Though we value none
But the horizontal one

W. H. Auden

Preface

Architecture is a visual art, like painting and sculpture. An architect, like a painter or sculptor, thinks in visual images – these are his art. And it is through them that he describes people and places in his buildings.

An architect is an imaginative being who leaves behind, as do the painter and sculptor, a visual imprint of his time, and future generations are able to use this to identify the nature of that time. But the fact that an architect is an artist is not so generally appreciated today as it should be; and this is, perhaps, a reason why Le Corbusier remains, for many people, an enigma.

There are other reasons. Probably the chief one is the vastness of architecture, for this means that it is an art that is difficult to comprehend. We can appreciate a chair, and the way its structure is put together and supported, because we can turn the chair over or sit on it. It is not so easy to apply the same sort of tests to a building because of its very size. And, while buildings are large, cities are even larger : here, before us, is an immensely elaborate patchwork threaded with a multiplicity of strands that lead in from all directions. At first it seems quite impossible to see a clear picture where there is, in fact, order, shape and continuity : all we see is a jumble. Yet it is at this point that one may make the discovery that the pattern is not possible to follow because a crucial piece of the jigsaw is missing; and that when this is placed in its correct position the surrounding jumble is suddenly transformed into a clear and complete picture. In Renaissance architecture we may turn to Andrea Palladio for the missing piece; in the twentieth century Le Corbusier provides it.

Once this precious piece of the puzzle has been picked

out, the magical properties lying inside the irregular outline of its edges can be explored. Then it will be possible to observe why Le Corbusier's work illuminates everything around it. This man was huge, like a continent; and his art was conceived on such a bewildering number of levels, and funded from so many associations and images, and from such a mass of historical material that it is not at all easy to recognize which door to open in the search for the correct route to the source of his inspiration. We can begin by putting down, with rapid strokes, some of the edges of his world. When these have been established the details can be filled in: these will show us the door. We have to start, as he always started, with a frame.

Le Corbusier said: 'It is human to err ...'

This was in the late 1950s – the finishing touches were being put to Sainte-Marie de la Tourette, his monastery outside Lyons. A very small window to a staircase – perhaps only fifteen centimetres square – had been built out of shape; the shuttering to the concrete had slipped. The foreman supervising the work was exceedingly worried. What would the Great Man say? He would be furious. But the foreman was wrong. Le Corbusier merely suggested that a plaque should be put under the window and inscribed with the words 'It is human to err'. He asked for no changes – the window could stay as it was. Perhaps it is a pity that he didn't go ahead with his plaque: the inscription would have been a good thought in a convent.

It is indeed human to err: mistakes are made, and about Le Corbusier, in particular, there have been an astonishing number. As great men go, and certainly great artists, he must be the most misunderstood of the century. Le Corbusier, an immensely human creature, made mistakes too; and those who fear change – and who oppose the true principles of modern architecture, striving to reject them in the erroneous belief that they are synonymous with all that is bad about the twentieth century (in the same way that nineteenth-century industrial buildings in their time were feared and rejected as architecture for much the same reason) – drag to the front, and out of context, the few mistakes that Le Corbusier may have made so that he can be condemned utterly, and blamed for what has gone wrong. This is a foolish mistake that grossly misjudges Le Corbusier. The attacks made – and criticism from English

journalists, architects and historians has been as bitter
as it has been ill-informed – reveal much more about the
attackers than the attacked. What good can be said of an
opposition that hammers on at Le Corbusier's historic pro-
nouncement that 'a house is a machine for living in' if it
fails, at the same time, to add what he said about the word
'functionalist' – 'this frightful word was born under other
skies than those I have always loved – those where the sun
reigns supreme'? Who will listen to the man who tries to
make a journalistic point by insinuating that Le Corbusier
chose to build villas for the rich, when it is known that Le
Corbusier cared nothing for material things, and started out
as a poor man having to accept the best offers going? In
any case, what does petty criticism matter when in the
next moment, and the next book, a photograph shows a
lovely staircase evaporating like breath through a roof into
a cloudless sky? It is customary for great artists to be attacked after death: in this century already Rodin has been
rejected as worthless, and Monet dropped completely out of
fashion.

Swiss-born in 1887, Le Corbusier was the highly complex
genius who led the architectural movement of the twentieth
century and devised realistic and imaginative solutions to
building problems in the face of hard materialism. His work
– his architecture, town planning schemes, paintings, drawings, sculpture and writings – must be seen together, and in
the context of both the past and his own times, if a true
picture of him is to be gained. Once some idea of what he
was really trying to do has been established, his buildings,
paintings, writings – not least his writings – can be enjoyed.
Like landmarks, his buildings peg out the development of a
life's work. He began when he was fifteen or so, worked his
way through cubism, reinforced concrete, whitewash,
houses and public buildings, and finally turned towards
nature. His work spread throughout the world, culminating
in the Corbusier Centre at Zurich – and everything for
which he struggled seems to be distilled there, in that single,

delicate little structure by the lake, completed after his death in 1965. For in this building his architecture, paintings, sculptures and writings are seen together, as they should be. The Centre is like a throwback to 1920 and *L'Esprit Nouveau*, a magazine for architecture, painting, music, science and poetry which Le Corbusier founded with his friend Ozenfant, the painter. The magazine made the same point as the Zurich Centre : the arts must be seen together, they cannot be separated without some loss of appreciation of each. The same is true for any understanding of Le Corbusier. The moment some part of his work is separated and examined in isolation – something he built, something he painted, something he wrote – and without reference to the multiplicity of other parts that were, however small, crucial fragments of the Le Corbusier mosaic, statements become loaded, mistakes are made and the unity of the total picture is disturbed. Some errors of judgement can be dismissed immediately, as they display plain ignorance or visual blindness. Others, however, are over-simplifications caused by an inability to get to grips with the immense depths of the artist; and limitations of experience are difficult obstacles to overcome in trying to make a true evaluation of this great man's art.

His work was like a flower. There were the roots embedded in the earth from which the plant grew, and through these feelers the nourishment was conveyed up the stem; and there was this beautiful thing which appeared like magic at the top to crown the energy that had gone into its making – a lovely shape, perfectly balanced, enclosing the most extraordinary details and collection of clear colours. Any part of this flower would make a fascinating study, all on its own – the petal, the pollen, the stigma, the stamen – but none would make real sense without an exact appreciation of the workings of the whole.

And so, to start with, there are Le Corbusier's roots. Three or four years ago, for instance, it suddenly seemed clear to me that Le Corbusier's real originality was to be found in his connections with ancient Greece; that he was an architect who could not be regarded solely in the context of his own century, or who could be tied to an aesthetic that was forced out by opportunities provided by mechanization and materials like reinforced concrete. Instead he was, like Andrea Palladio and Inigo Jones before him, an architect who must be related to architectural disciplines and principles worked out in Athens more than two thousand years ago. He was an architect who accepted these disciplines and principles as the foundations from which to start his work. Le Corbusier made adjustments to these disciplines and principles only in so far as they were required to meet the conditions of his own time.

The decision to make these adjustments shows no departure from the pattern of history. Inigo Jones, for example, said, 'One must first design the ground, as it is for use, and then vary and adorn it. Compose it with decorum, according to its use and the order of the architecture to which it belongs.' Le Corbusier's order of architecture was, of course, very different from Jones's – the enormous technological advances that had taken place in the nineteenth century, and were rapidly continuing to take place, had to be absorbed within the disciplines of the classical method. But these disciplines still held good: they remained the same as people remain the same. Le Corbusier described the disciplines as 'the regulating lines' and as 'the rules which order'. Unlike Frank Lloyd Wright, the modern American architect, who had little outside nature to start from, Le Corbusier had the whole of western culture before and behind him, from which to learn; and it was partly because he did learn from it, and did not abandon it, that he became the undisputed leader of the modern architectural movement. Since he accepted tradition as part of himself there was no resistance from it, and he felt free to put it to work using new forms which gave it a different range. Tradition was not there to block progress: it was a safe-deposit of knowledge and experience to be consulted when needed. At a very early age, following much the same trail that Palladio and Jones had followed when they were young, Le Corbusier had gone back into the past; he had explored Paris, Italy, the Greek islands, he had seen the Parthenon. By the age of twenty he was, to use words applied to Jones in his time, 'a great traveller'. Thus, like Palladio and Jones, Le Corbusier was in a position to select from the past what was still relevant to the present, to extract the essence and reject the bulk; like Palladio and Jones, he boiled architecture down to the bones. He took the cube as a form to start from, and used it and its different combinations in a new way with new materials; he went back to the Greek diagram of proportion and employed its aesthetic system of parts to relate the size of his buildings to the proportion and size of human beings. Seen from this angle and distance, Le Corbusier's work could be regarded simply as a continuation of the classical tradition. Yet he set out to replace the old with something new, but not in such a way as to deny the new the benefit of the knowledge and wisdom of classical experience. Correspondingly, in bringing enlightenment to tradition he was assisting tradition to progress and renew itself.

Now this realization led to the possibility of comprehending Le Corbusier's work in a different way – those houses he built in the 1920s (Villas La Roche, Cook, Stein and Savoye) were changed by the identification of their origins. Previously, for me, these superb works of architecture were fixed in the mind as inventions, which they were: they rediscovered architecture at a time when there was nothing but dying academicism, imitation and lethargy, and they gave a new generation of architects the confidence to think for themselves again, and to create where before they had merely copied. Yet the wonder with which we look back at these buildings by Le Corbusier is only increased by the knowledge of their intimate connections with ancient Greek architecture, the awareness that the

roots for this early modern white style lay there, in Athens.
The pleasure communicated by Le Corbusier's early magic is
thereby intensified. The ramps, the corkscrew staircases, the
balconies, the shapes of forms extended into the air by the
lines of handrails thin as hair, the outbreaks of curves in his
beautiful plans – the plans of corridors, flights of steps, bathrooms and other details – seem suddenly to possess an un-
usual freedom once the significance of the cube's frame
containing them has been properly observed. With this observation, moreover, one of Le Corbusier's secrets has been
revealed, thus disclosing a secret common to all architecture. The forms within the frame emerge with a greater
vigour, as people feel a greater sense of freedom when their
surroundings preserve order. And once observed, the presence of this order in the cube correspondingly emerges with
a greater authority, where before it was scarcely noticed.
Yet, again, the reticence of the frame was part of the power
of a Le Corbusier building: this reticence, when combined
with a single architectural statement of extreme simplicity,
accepted the modern and daring opportunities upon which
Le Corbusier thrived – the release of space, the remarkable
acrobatics of reinforced concrete – as it accepted human
muddle and mistakes, like the foreman's window at La
Tourette.

With this knowledge of his classical roots, a few pieces
of the highly complicated mosaic fall into place: we know
more about the life of the 'flower'. And we make the discovery, too, that his architecture has a perfectly comprehensible humanism and commonsense, and that the magic
of the architecture is the more poetic because of this
humanism and commonsense. It ought to be possible, one
feels, to make these discoveries immediately upon opening
his own books on his work: his aims are clearly enough
stated. He said to a reporter from an English Sunday news-
paper in 1965, a month before he died: 'Everything is in
my books – if you want to know what I think read them –

it is all there.' Of course this is true, yet one sympathizes with the reporter if he felt confused.

Without a detailed knowledge and understanding of Le Corbusier's work as a whole, it is difficult, if not impossible, to relate what he wrote to what he did. While the books describe the roots and the aims they are also part of the 'flower'. They are works of genius in themselves, as fresh and exciting as his buildings, and there are moments of sheer poetry – his descriptions of places and ideas could be as clear and bright as a cloudless sky where 'the sun reigns supreme'. But although his meaning often remains obscure without constant cross-references to his buildings, drawings and paintings, he was, of course, correct to stress the tremendous importance of his writing because this was his most powerful propaganda weapon. It was his books, far more than his buildings, that broke through the stubborn defences set up by prejudice, that encircled the philistines and spread the architectural modern gospel throughout the world. His books, like those by Palladio and Serlio in the sixteenth century, were best-sellers, and it is in the first volume of the famous series of collections of his work (*Oeuvre Complète*), covering the period 1910 to 1929, that he set down his faith in classical principles. This book really starts with a design for some artists' studios in 1910 (*see Plate 3*). In this a sequence of cubes (the studios) is separated by courtyards and arranged round a pyramid : a total composition is contained within the outline of a square plan. All the forms had ancient origins, each had a symmetrical geometry, yet, set out in this way, the forms were freed – the larger, complete order of the square stressed the individuality of the parts, so that the whole was greater than the sum of these parts. In this book, too, there were diagrams which related to the cube as he used it in his first houses : he described his spreading plan for the Villa La Roche as 'easiest', and the double cube of the Villa Stein as 'very difficult', and the cube form outlined by columns at his house in Stuttgart as 'very easy', and the Villa Savoye – which was a distillation of conclusions reached in the preceding three designs – as 'very generous'. Like the artists' studios of 1910, the total composition of the Villa Savoye, built twenty years later, was contained within a square plan.

Then, in *Towards a New Architecture*, also published in the 1920s, Le Corbusier throws all the ingredients of the twentieth century together. The constructional modules used by early people : the geometry of the Golden Section shown in the façade of the Arsenal of Piraeus, the Capitol in Rome, the Petit Trianon in Versailles, the front of Notre Dame; the inspiration of ship, aeroplane and car design, of mass-production and mechanization. Lying in the background, giving order and continuity to this remarkable range of ideas, projects and happenings, is man and his manifestation in the classical frame : it is this frame which holds the theme of Le Corbusier's book together. The infinitely delicate ink drawings of the Atriums at Pompeii and Hadrian's Villa, the photographs of the Propylea and of the Parthenon (taken when Le Corbusier was only nineteen or twenty) in which the columns select the extent of the view, describe the background order provided by the frame. Le Corbusier is not giving us historical facts : he is giving us visual information, reminding us all the time that an underlying order that is present in nature is – as it always has been – required by people. 'There is no such thing as primitive man,' he writes in *Towards a New Architecture*, 'there are primitive resources. The idea is constant. . . .' Once the notion of mere historical fact is dismissed from the picture, the real processes of evolution come more clearly into view, and it becomes possible to see how ideas that have been developed in the past can, if applicable, be used in the present. Once it becomes possible to see why certain things were done in the past, it then becomes possible to see how such things relate to the present. It is possible, for instance, to observe the connections between the architectural conceptions of ancient Greece and Le Corbusier's Villa Savoye, his *Pavillon Suisse* and his Centre in Zurich. These connections are clear, as clear as the architectural statements the buildings set down before us. As in the past, a total unity is achieved and this gives the conceptions their order: and once there is order there is freedom to discover what is possible within that order.

Thus it follows that the past and the present, the traditional and truly contemporary architectural styles, the ancient Greek and Le Corbusier, cannot really be considered as separate beings at all. They are, in reality, part of each other, such that, over the distance of time, neither could have a living existence without the other. It follows, too, that art is not made in a vacuum but merely has its place in the continuum, and that it is this continuum which, in fact, frames the whole story from the ancient Greeks to Le Corbusier. In building, the frame shows itself in proportion and shape, in the application of the circle and the square, in a proper relationship of the parts, and in the ways in which the properties of these forms and parts are related to the scale of people. This is how ordered surroundings grow, but they are also surroundings that are, to an extent, unfinished, and it is for this reason that people feel comfortable in them, and sufficiently at ease to make their own contribution to them. This was Le Corbusier's point: he stresses it in *Towards a New Architecture*.

Yet for all this the connection between the books and the buildings may remain unclear. For one thing the media of writing and architecture are so different that it is difficult to make the intellectual or visual leap. Again, lack of experience and knowledge sets up what appear to be insuperable barriers. There is still an enormous amount of excavation to be done if the meaning of his buildings is to be exposed. Le Corbusier picked up – yes, you could say that – where the Greeks left off, and it was the classical background that influenced the form of, for example, the Villa Savoye. But this background included the work of Cézanne, the source of a movement in painting that ran parallel to modern architecture, and from which flowed the ideas of artists like Léger,

Braque, Gris and Picasso. There is a picture by Cézanne titled the *Pigeon Tower at Bellevue* which seems to suggest an association of ideas. It was painted two years after Le Corbusier was born and it is specially interesting because the tower bears an unmistakable likeness to the light shafts at the Chapel at Ronchamp that Le Corbusier designed and built in the 1950s, a building which may well be described as his most original work. The first thought that comes to mind is perhaps somewhat naive: had Le Corbusier been inspired by this painting? Had the cubist form of the tower put a shape into his head? The ideas of an era overlap: to gain a mental picture of the era, we have to approach it in the same way that we have to approach Le Corbusier himself. All available material – architecture, science, painting, sculpture, poetry – must be sifted and studied, and the relationships observed. And it is the combined impact of all available material that leaves the imprint by which the era, like any other before it, may be identified. For instance, one of Picasso's constructions of a man – the egg-crate head, the lump of stone for a body supported on legs of two columns – bears a startling resemblance to some views of the form and appearance of Le Corbusier's monastery of La Tourette (*see Plate 23*). The *Pigeon Tower*, although painted earlier, was a fragment of the same picture, of the same shared vision.

Was this the truth – had Le Corbusier shared a vision with Cézanne? The likeness between the tower and the light shaft is, after all, quite remarkable. But if this is true, it is only true because of their shared devotion to cubism. For while it is true in so far as their language was much the same – they both worked and talked in terms of cubes, cones and cylinders – Le Corbusier's cylindrical imagery was also derived from other things around him, like the funnels and ventilators of ships – ships were a most important source of inspiration. Then again, it has to be remembered that the light shaft was only one element among many at the Chapel: the form of the building itself seems to fit an entirely different jigsaw. But what jigsaw? And at this point one remembers the Picasso man; the resemblance between this and the Le Corbusier convent has a much simpler explanation, and a more profound meaning, than that offered by the suggestion of direct contemporary influences. Here both artists were working from people: both works describe people – or, to be exact, one describes a man, the other a group of men. Picasso's construction is a startlingly vivid representation of a man. But so, too, is the convent a vivid representation of men, grouped together: the double storey of monks' cells at the top of the structure are the eyes which see across to the hills to the north, the weighty part at the centre contains the communal spaces for meeting, eating and reading, and the columns below are the legs that raise the building up so that the monks can look beyond their immediate earthly boundaries – the sloping hillside of long grass. This comparison brings the truth into much sharper focus: architecture describes people, and Picasso's man helps us to make this discovery. And a visit to southern France can help to clear up the mysterious connection between Cézanne and Le Corbusier, and so suggest some leads about the origin of the Chapel's form.

On a local bus that was going from Alba in the Ardèche to Orange in Provence, and with a stone holiday house that Le Corbusier built just before the 1939 war fixed, for some reason, very clearly in my mind, I suddenly noticed a traditional storehouse in a hollow. Now the surprising thing about this storehouse was the great similarity of its shape and general appearance to the Le Corbusier Chapel at Ronchamp. The roof turned up at the end (rather like the prow of a canoe) and the walls came to a point below making, presumably, a roughly triangular plan; and small windows of different sizes were scattered over the stone sides. Surely this was it, this storehouse was the source of Le Corbusier's inspiration? The sense of discovery was so astonishing that one felt like an archaeologist who has just dug up some ancient remains, the identification of which will change the dates of an early civilization by several thousand years. The presence of Le Corbusier suddenly seemed extremely close : it was just as though he had passed this way on the same bus only the other day. Here was the material from which he had been working – a local style in the depths of rural France – much the same material from which Cézanne, too, had been working. Hence the similarities. For the storehouse was not, in reality, Le Corbusier's sole source of inspiration – this became clear when the storehouse made you look closely at the rural style, to sink more deeply into it, to become more aware : in particular, the shape of the chapel seemed to embody the generous breadth of buildings in the locality, the gentle slopes of their roofs, characteristics that are again noticeable at Le Thoronet, the abbey which was not far away and which fascinated Le Corbusier. You forget, for the time being, the *Pigeon Tower*. Immediately the Chapel took on a new meaning for me, as the Villa Savoye had when its classical origins became plain, and as Cézanne's olive trees and cart tracks do once the places where he painted are known : Van Gogh's pictures of rocks and clouds are landscapes of the imagination before the mountains of Provence have been seen. This natural material was another part of Le Corbusier's roots that nourished the 'flower'. The illusion of influences – of Cézanne, of even perhaps Japan – seemed suddenly crude, almost nonsensical; they vanished for that moment into oblivion. The truth was as simple as it was profound. Like Picasso, Le Corbusier worked from people; but, like Cézanne, he also worked from the place.

Now we begin to get a glimmer of the extreme complexity of a Le Corbusier building. In a sense it is autobiographical, as it must be for a lifetime's experience is embedded in the Chapel at Ronchamp. There are the memories of the Greek island villages which the architect saw in his early travels; the scattering of openings on sunny white backgrounds coincides with the rough irregular imagery of French peasant architecture; there is the ghost of the classi-

cal past in the single clean statement of the sculptural object on the top of a hill; there is the freedom of nature and
the painter in the interlocking, overlapping, sweeping walls
of the superb plan. Simultaneously, this building is as
French as the smell of gauloises in the Métro – it could be
nowhere but France, the country Le Corbusier made his
home. And so we make other discoveries : the experience in
the Ardèche didn't end with the storehouse. But the recog-
nition of the storehouse (and peasant architecture in general) as a possible part of Le Corbusier's material had the
effect of making one see the surroundings through the
architect's eyes, and, for this reason, the surroundings constantly revived images of his work – and not just of his
buildings, but his paintings and drawings as well. It was the
stone of the farm buildings, like the nougat of the district,
which recalled the holiday house of the late 1930s, and the
framed view of a valley between the fortifications of a
château gateway seemed to resemble exactly the architect's
tiny ink sketches where the notes about the properties of a
place are ringed by the clouds' edges; and some plaster that
had dropped off a nearby wall left behind a shape in the
pock-marked cement that had an uncanny likeness to the
floating figures of his later pictures. And so the closer you
look, the less easy it becomes to dissociate the Chapel at
Ronchamp from the architecture of its southern surroundings. If you allow your eye a wider range it will begin to
take in all kinds of characteristics that belong to Provence :
forms seen in abbeys like Le Thoronet and Sénanque, the
vigorous water spouts and stone tiles of Venasque's church
and its Byzantine baptistry. This was Le Corbusier's material, quite as much as it was Cézanne's. The clarity with
which such associations are transmitted indicates the life
that lay beyond Le Corbusier's works of art, and far beyond, too, his rediscoveries of classical principles and the
conquest of modern technology. At that moment, in the
Ardèche, and later in Provence, it seemed plain that all he
had striven for in the early years was really a foundation

for a much more ambitious adventure – for a voyage, as he put it once, 'of discovery into the inexhaustible domain of Nature', and with it the recovery of an indigenous architecture. For since he was working with the materials of a country, he must also have been seeking to disclose the properties of these materials in his buildings.

This gives his work another dimension. Within the limitations of individual projects and buildings, Le Corbusier set out to achieve, single-handed and in the space of a lifetime, what preceding cultures had accomplished over innumerable generations. Having established principles of design derived from classical and modern sources, he continued with a search to develop the indigenous nature of the country in which he was working. In other words, he was restricted by the cube and the machine while he was trying to understand their possibilities. Once he did understand both, he could control them, and was in a sense free of them. In this way, therefore, he found a harmony between new and old (and the search for harmony was, he said, 'the noblest of human passions') and brought enlightenment to tradition – a single achievement which appears to place him above any architect who preceded him.

This search for an architecture with a more universal range, that was concerned with the day-to-day rhythm of life, was not accompanied, however, by any loss of respect for earlier objectives. Le Corbusier's sights were held exactly in focus on every facet of architecture, all the time: not for one moment did he relax his vigilance to protect the integrity of the total architectural objective. The free plan, for instance, of sweeping walls at the Ronchamp Chapel was not throwing a spanner in the classical works. The frame was as firmly stressed as ever. Le Corbusier was merely taking a leaf out of nature's notebook and showing the world that frames do not have to be square or rectangular – such forms simply demonstrate the limitations of human knowledge and building methods – but that they can, like the trunks of trees which enclose an exquisite view, be any shape, provided of course that the aesthetic and practical objectives are met. After all, natural forms were the roots of ancient Greek architecture in the first place.

It is often impossible to imagine how Le Corbusier accomplished so much, how he did it all – built so many buildings, designed so many more, conceived schemes for cities, painted ceaselessly, travelled and drew the whole time (even from trains and aeroplanes), made sculpture, wrote the books which he also designed. It was almost as though there was a committee of people in his head who worked in perfect harmony together, and that they were all geniuses in their own line.

But how did he *really* work? For a start, intensely hard and with absolute consistency – he was the kind of man you would expect to find up, and thinking with total clarity, at six o'clock every morning. His concentration was as exceptional as his ability to assess all the diverse aspects of a problem was fast: he could listen to four or five conversations going on at once and then, drawing with coloured pencils, reproduce what had been said as a diagram that resolved the discussion in precise building terms. 'What you mean,' he would comment, 'is *this*.' A problem, he would say, had to be correctly posed if it was to be correctly solved. Drawing was, of course, his most natural and vivid method of expression. Diagrams describing a myriad of ideas were often carried out on an enormous blackboard at Rue de Sèvres – this blackboard was one of the most memorable features at the studio where his building design was done. On it he would show a client for, say, a house a full-size section through a room, and, because the section *was* full-size, it had an immediacy that made the person feel that he was in that room: it was already a living being. The height of the room was, perhaps, drawn at two metres – one of Le Corbusier's favourite dimensions. The client might think that the height was too low, claustrophobic – he didn't understand the extent of the excitement generated by a low ceiling surface when it is seen in the context of the space of landscape beyond the long horizontal windows of, for instance, the Villa Stein, and when experienced next to a double storey volume. Le Corbusier would shrug off the criticism with another drawing that raised the ceiling by a few centimetres. His diagram was more than a description of a particular house for a particular person; it was a description of the immense opportunities offered by modern architecture, and of the poetry of ideas.

At the same time Le Corbusier gathered around himself a circle of collaborators who were, in their different ways, like him. They shared the same interests, and, after working with him, they became to a degree projections of himself. These people were naturally attracted to Le Corbusier and his genius, and were simultaneously as much a source of inspiration to him as was nature and as the fir trees round his birth-place in the Jura mountains, the sea-shells, fossils and shape of women. The collaborators shared Le Corbusier's vision but they were also remarkable artists in areas of work which centred, in every case, on craftsmanship : Le Corbusier felt very happy and relaxed with craftsmen – perhaps this was because his father had been a very fine one, and because he had been brought up among them. Working with Le Corbusier there was Pierre Jeanneret, his cousin and faithful administrator; Prouvé, the engineer and specialist in prefabrication; Hervé, the photographer and observing eye; Xenakis, the composer and engineer; Savina, the sculptor, who made the benches at Ronchamp with his own hands; Jacques Michel, the architect who carried through the Jaoul house in Neuilly on the outskirts of Paris. There were many others, particularly among the craftsmen who were responsible for the parts of his buildings; some of Le Corbusier's happiest moments when he designed and built the Chapel at Ronchamp were spent with the blacksmith Méchinaul, who wrought the handrails for him. It was through inspired collaborators like these that Le Corbusier worked. Their dedication and labour meant, it seems, that Le Corbusier himself was able to pursue, undisturbed, all the innumerable matters that were central to his art.

It was in the struggle to unite his own extraordinary gifts – those of engineer and painter – and in the realization of a perfect union between the two, that Le Corbusier re-invented architecture. Before he arrived on the scene, back in the early 1920s, there was nothing for architects to follow with certainty because there was no one to show them the way. From that moment until the end of his life, Le Corbusier remained by far the most exciting architect of the twentieth century.

It is natural, possibly, to think of the combined range of Le Corbusier and Frank Lloyd Wright as representative of the total image of modern architecture. These two architects started off from widely differing philosophies: Le Corbusier's was derived from the western point of view, Wright's was strongly based on the eastern admiration for nature where landscape was regarded as more important than building. As time went on, however, and the experience of both architects increased, the gap which separated their architectures gradually narrowed, until they seemed to merge. Le Corbusier became more deeply interested in nature and what could be learnt from natural forms, and Wright, through the growing contact across the Atlantic with an accompanying exchange of ideas, became more influenced by western forms. Yet this view, interesting enough in its way, can be over-simplified. Wright is closely associated with Japanese architecture through the houses he built in the first years of the century, but one should not forget that Le Corbusier also visited the Orient. There are his drawings of Chinese houses, and from the earliest days he was aware of natural forms. He writes: 'My childhood years were spent with my companions, in nature. I have learned how the flowers were, inside and out, the form and colour of birds. I understood how a tree grows and why it keeps its balance even in the midst of a storm. The tree, friend of man, symbol of all organic creation; the trees, image of a total construction. . . .' Lloyd Wright talked about trees in a very similar fashion. He said that they were 'like various, beautiful buildings, of more different kinds than all the architectures of the world'. Both architects had spent their childhoods near the land, but Le Corbusier got to grips with the classical background long before Wright was aware either of its existence or importance. Le Corbusier chose to put it first, before the study of nature, because he required the clarity of the classical vision as a starting point. The vision regulated his life. It follows, therefore, that when Le Corbusier did eventually turn towards nature for further inspiration the range of his work encompassed the whole of architecture, of the combined influences of east and west, of all the forces that may act simultaneously on a building; and from this work we can gain a clearer picture of architecture than we would from a study of the combined work of Le Corbusier and Wright. For it was Le Corbusier, more than Wright, who managed to keep all the balls in the air at the same time.

He was, above all else, a great creator. He was an artist who loved making things. The various names that have been pinned to him – anything from 'functionalist' to 'sociologist' – and which, in a curious way, seem to be devised to reduce the true stature of his work and to undermine his position as an artist, are all wrong. His output equalled Picasso's, and was as varied : it is truly amazing that he filled his life with so much that is memorable. Everything he used, or made, came alive – a pencil line, the carefree line of a stair or an arch, a roof-line, the rounded lines of a bath and the curved wall that outlined its shape. He was like a magician. On the one hand he possessed that close friendship with the past which suggests that his existence was at least his second or third on earth. The Parthenon seemed to be something he had grown up with, as though it was the church at the end of his street; Michelangelo was a person he knew and understood, like the fellow next door; and the mandala, the geometric form and eastern symbol of balance that makes an appearance again and again in his buildings and paintings, came as second nature to him, like an archetype. Yet at the same time he seemed to have the power to produce something from nothing. Take the Villa Savoye: this is an extraordinary invention. The long, low, white object stranded in a field of tall grass; the sun terrace with its innovatory concrete breakfast table and ramps were unique – spacious and unexpected as they are, they give enormous pleasure (*see Plate 1*). But then you look again and make the discovery that Le Corbusier has not really produced something from nothing; that the villa is an architectural solution to an aesthetic problem fundamental to all building. The problem was uncovered when he was working on the cube at the Villa La Roche. One of the aims there was a free, open plan that followed the movements of people. But could that freedom of movement be achieved within an acceptable aesthetic order? This was the architectural problem. Le Corbusier studied it as a painter studies a model, minutely, from different points of view, so that the conclusions set down at the Villas La Roche, Stein and Savoye appear to represent the various facets of the same problem. He did not seem satisfied by La Roche, describing it as 'easiest'. But then, one feels, he was not entirely satisfied with the Stein house at Garches. He studied the problem again at the Stuttgart house, for in principle, as the diagram shows, the use of a structural frame should free the plan. And so to Poissy and the Villa Savoye; and here is the answer. Le Corbusier puts a frame round a plan that has the irregularity of La Roche; the space that is left over becomes a sun terrace; and the whole structure is lifted up on *piloti* to get both the best of the view and the aesthetic solution to the problem. Thus he finally achieved a plan that follows the natural movements of people within the architectural frame of a square or wall. The interior terrace merely follows the shapes of rooms – living spaces, bedrooms, study:

the plan is a description of private actions and behaviour once people are inside a house.

The artist is at work: good buildings come from people, and people are the artist's material. But architecture is like a double image. In one image there is just a set of rooms, materials, colour and things like cupboards. In the second image the set of rooms, the materials, the colour and so on are seen in abstract terms. Somewhere between the two images, and encompassing the whole composition, is the atmosphere, the imagination, balance – a glimpse of the perfect life. As a painter or a poet might, Le Corbusier captures the universal romantic dream at the Villa Savoye – to lie down and look at blue skies through green leaves – and something of the warmth of the lakeside house he built for his parents in 1923 wafts in with the bees, the butterflies and the scent of creepers and flowers through the opening on to the privacy of the terrace as the ramp slopes back restfully. Now you are at the centre of the Le Corbusier world, mesmerized by his imagination, the generosity of his spaces, his love of sunlight and air – the idyllic world: this is the world that the Villa Savoye captures within its frame, and it does so because Le Corbusier has composed the house as a poem. Like the poet or painter, he is showing us a way of looking at ordinary things which we did not see before. Architecture is like a painting, but a painting through which we walk. Like Klee's description of a painting, we wander about in a building and then we leave it. Thus it is near to sculpture. Braque, for instance, paints a picture where a river valley breaks through a single gap in the white cliffs at Verangeville to the space of the sands and the sea beyond; in a Le Corbusier building you may experience the kind of gap which Braque described, and you walk through it to the space of the landscape or city beyond. Le Corbusier himself said, 'But where does sculpture begin, where does painting begin, where does architecture begin?' These words recall Cézanne's, who said that it took him 'forty years to realize that painting was not sculpture'.

There is no question that the Villa Savoye had a very special magnetism. It was not only the successful climax of the first phase of Le Corbusier's work, it also, as much as anything else that he did, broke through the barriers of prejudice and spread the white style of architecture throughout Europe. Le Corbusier had passed on his inspiration to others; art is truth and it connects with the world; his buildings were a mirror of an image outside himself. Just as Le Corbusier drew his ideas from everything around him, so his contemporaries and followers drew their ideas from him. One example is the effect that the Villa Savoye had on an English artist, Christopher Wood, who painted the house and put a zebra in the sun terrace, turning the scene into something from Africa (*See Plate 2*). It was a beautiful painting, one of the best he ever did, and all the more remarkable because the house was barely finished when Wood came upon it. Of course he must have been carried away by the strangeness of the design, but it is extraordinary, nevertheless, that the imagination of the place was transmitted with such speed and freshness that a younger artist was able to make a fully achieved picture from what he saw. No other modern architectural work has inspired a painter in this way: *The Zebra with the Parachute* is a unique affirmation of the power of Le Corbusier's genius. The point of the building had gone right home, and the warmth, the space, the airiness and light which Le Corbusier had spread through its construction reappeared as a hot, mysterious oasis with a back-drop of white walls, turrets and ramps – as a mirage, perhaps. So, in a way, the painting is a portrait of an idea, and Wood perpetuated this idea in another form. The idea of the painting is the same as the idea that Le Corbusier captured in his sun-terrace – the remembered pleasure, if you like, of a single timeless moment in the sun one afternoon – and the peculiar presence of the zebra catches, as somehow no human figure could, the mood of that moment.

And so Le Corbusier put an idea into Wood's head, as a

storehouse perhaps put an idea into Le Corbusier's head : the precise eye of the artist reacts to different situations according to needs. But if the storehouse does present a reference for the inspiration of the chapel at Ronchamp it should be regarded as little more than a footnote. Le Corbusier himself compared the roof at Ronchamp to the shell of a crab he picked up on a visit to New York; he says that this shell inspired both the shape and structure of the roof. This does not mean that some particle of rural architecture does not form a piece of the elaborate mosaic. On the other hand, the image of the seashell connects with another attributed to Le Corbusier, and this was that the underside of the roof was like the underside of a boat. This is very interesting. For one thing, there is the succession of beautiful photographs by Lucien Hervé which shows the chapel appearing over the crest of a hill like the billowing sail of a ship – sometimes we are shown just the tip of the sail, sometimes the whole of it; the white walls and the roof make the sail – together, as two separate elements, they belong as one image in which the magnificence of a sail grandly riding a wave in the fluttering freshness of a sea breeze is clearly suggested : the sail even seems to be in movement (*see Plate 4*). This image is not unreasonable in view of Le Corbusier's love of the sea and ships : some of his early designs, the enormous length of the horizontal windows at the Villas Stein and Savoye, and the later roof superstructure of *L'Unité d'Habitation* owe a good deal to the deck, bridge and balcony architecture of liners. But these associations take quite a different turn at Ronchamp. In this building the imagery is less literal, far more relaxed : and the picture of a boat in full sail seems to hold, exactly in focus, the freedom he found in the work of his last twenty years after the war.

Inside, one is under the boat; here, there are other sensations. Le Corbusier was very interested in acoustics; both his mother and brother were musicians, and so was Le Corbusier in his way – his buildings displayed a total allegiance to the musical conception of a discipline and its variations, the beat and its improvisations. He described the undulating walls at Ronchamp as 'visual acoustics' – this recalls valleys and hollows, and rebounding echoes heard in valleys and hollows; suggesting, too, the softness, roundness and changing contours of nature. And he pointed out, again, that the roof at Ronchamp was a good acoustic shape. It muffles sound, so that the presence of quiet is truly found inside the chapel. Yet you are aware of its presence because, when you listen, you are also aware of the existence of distant sounds like those of the sea heard in a shell. These sounds seem to pick up other messages. You are under the boat and its underside is supported on those triangular props of the boat yards. The illusion is intensified by the triangular walls of the church with its deep window recesses where the sun gleams through the oranges, yellows and blues of Le Corbusier's coloured glass, and by the light that reaches the interior from the shafts. The structure, concealed behind the rough white plaster coatings, is triangular, like the boat props, but the illusion of the props is conveyed solely by the shape of the walls which slope away to a point at the top. Suddenly, and very slowly, you seem to be following Le Corbusier's train of thought, even perhaps the hand which made the early smudgy pencil drawings describing, with a series of unique architectural shapes, the form and plan of the Chapel (*see Plate 5*). The inside, when you come to look at it, is like the kind of random space that might be made when a boat is propped up over a rock-pool on a beach, but the rock-pool has been enlarged to the size of a lake. This image of life in the rock-pool suggests itself because Le Corbusier had an extraordinarily exact eye for minutiae, for the microscopic details of existence, of flowers, birds and butterflies; he saw the connections between nature and the human world, and Ronchamp suggests he has put some image like a rock-pool under a magnifying glass. The shapes which make the enclosure of the interior have a mixed complexity and freedom that indicate that there are natural laws at work: they have the spontaneity of a stream. The rounded forms of the plan might be a sketch of a pool by the seaside framed by large stones. If you then imagine that you are a tiny insect moving between the stones, you can see that the stones, to these insects, might be like the rounded shapes that you find at Ronchamp; that the light, filtering into the pool between the stones and the roof of the boat overhead, might be like the shafted sunshine let in from above; and that the presence of stillness and quiet that is felt in the Chapel might well resemble the immunity from the world possessed by the remote life in the rock-pool.

And then, at this point, you make another discovery. You have noticed that the imagery of the church with its billowing forms and expansive plan has a likeness to pictures of sails and boats and pools. Now there could be another reason for this which does not stem simply from a transmission of visual associations. The shape of a sail is produced by a wind blowing; there is a physical, and thus visual, connection between the strength of the wind and the shape of the sail – the sail is restraining the force of the wind when it is completely filled. In the same way water fills any corner it can find, spreading into every crevice, until the pool is finally contained by a cliff of pebbles. These natural laws seem to be at work at Ronchamp too. When the entering eye scans the interior of the Chapel it does not, so to speak, go round in circles, which it would do if it was confronted with straight, flat walls, and a flat ceiling that met a wall with a right-angle. Instead, as the the wind fills the sail, the eye is able to wander, to look beyond the objects like the large stones of the rock-pool, and into corners and spaces beyond and behind the objects, and to follow the light up towards the sky above the roof. It is only when the limit of the space is reached that the flowing walls restrain the eye.

Yet when you then turn up a drawing by Le Corbusier of a plan of a Greek temple you may find that it seems to have a puzzling likeness to the plan at Ronchamp. The Greek plan is, of course, rectangular, but the naturalness with which the shapes of the temples are made is somehow essentially the same as the naturalness of the forms at Ronchamp. Again, this association of ideas is, like others, uncanny – Le Corbusier's chapel is, after all, a free, asymmetrical shape. There is, and not unreasonably, the likelihood that the character and spatial properties of the Greek plans underwent some sort of change in Le Corbusier's representation of them : if a painter makes a drawing of a cow, for example, he introduces something of himself into his representation of this cow. In other words, Le Corbusier was already, perhaps, toying with the opportunities he could see in the temple's plan while he was making the drawing. Nevertheless, he wouldn't falsify historic material; like the painter who draws the cow, he would always be honest, always exact – without truth and accuracy nothing at all can succeed. But what he did do in his drawings – as his pictures of Hadrian's Villa and Pompeii show – was to extract and stress what was of aesthetic and architectural importance, and what had a spatial and structural meaning, so demonstrating that ideas of the far distant past can, if observed correctly, teach us how to build today. He is showing us a way of looking at architectural history that will help us to understand it properly. In doing so, he brings it suddenly to life.

With the drawing of the temple, however, another association tightens into focus. The Greeks had conceived their buildings as a precise and coherent relationship of architectural parts, the entire composition of which then relates to the outside world. Le Corbusier accepted this conception of architecture absolutely, and at Ronchamp he saw his chapel as he saw his work as a whole – as a fragment of something that was infinitely larger : he had perceived its relationship to the world around it. When he was young and on his travels, he had seen the peasant (or, as he called it, 'folk') architecture of the Greek islands, and the irregular jumble of their villages : if Le Corbusier had some special secret source of inspiration it was on these islands. Although no familiar architectural frame exists for this jumble, it is, nevertheless, an exceedingly beautiful jumble: the picture made is perfect and complete. It is easy to see why this island architecture so inspired Le Corbusier. 'Consider the surface of the waters,' he said. 'Consider also the entire world rounded by the azure sky....' For there is a frame for this architecture, a frame which resides in the strong and regular blues of the sea and the sky, and it is against these that the little collections of white buildings are constantly seen; and so large and dependable is this frame that any kind of irregularity and scattering of detail in white walls, random openings, church towers and roofs fall naturally into place; right and necessary, whatever the situation. When Le Corbusier said that what this architecture required was organization, he meant that he had seen in it possibilities that could be used in another way when transferred to another place with a different climate. The complexity of the detail and the simplicity of the natural frame had, in other words, an underlying meaning that could be exploited elsewhere. And so, possibly, it is with this association of ideas, making a simultaneous connection with innumerable other associations and images, that the imaginative secret of Ronchamp really lies: nature was the root from which the flower bloomed. Le Corbusier had already decided that an architectural frame did not have to be square or rectangular, in the same way that he discovered at his monastery of La Tourette that the vertical divisions of windows did not necessarily have to be placed at equal intervals. And when his chapel is seen in relation to the outside world, you find that it is the green loveliness of nature which is the frame, and that it is the countryside that seems to have insisted upon the chapel's irregularities and free forms, and upon the 'visual acoustics'. The plan alone has all the accidental casualness of the profile of a Greek island village. Le Corbusier says it best: 'A respectable personality was nevertheless present, which was the landscape, the four horizons. It was they who commanded.'

Le Corbusier's real name was Charles-Edouard Jeanneret. He was an inventor and he invented a name. Like everything else he invented, the name (which means 'crow-like') somehow describes him. What pleased him most, apparently, was the sound of the name, and he adopted it as a pseudonym when he was writing for *L'Esprit Nouveau* after the First World War.

He was born at La Chaux-de-Fonds, a world centre for clock making, just on the Swiss side of the border with France, a small town three thousand feet up in the Jura mountains in a district that has, for a long time, wanted independence from Switzerland. Knowledge about his early background is sketchy but the facts that there are should be noted. His father had an enamelling business and was also a great mountaineer – for most of his life he was president of the Swiss mountaineers' association. His mother was a musician and lived to a hundred-and-one. His elder brother was a well-known violinist and composer, and his cousin, Pierre, became his partner. It is clear that the family had energy and stamina, and that its natural gifts were strongly inclined towards art and craftsmanship. Le Corbusier shared all the energies of his parents but used them differently. Indeed they were necessary for him to break through the philistinism and narrow-mindedness of his time, to withstand the vicious criticism of his ideas, to maintain his tremendous output of work, and to protect his art in the face of a rapidly growing crisis of materialism.

As a boy he roamed round the countryside, examining it. He was always drawing, and the early sketches and paintings reproduced in his books were remarkable, particularly those of his 'companions in nature' like the fir trees with their snow-laden boughs; it was in these he first noticed the outline of a beautiful shape that stayed with him for ever, and reappeared years later in his building forms. He left school at thirteen-and-a-half and went to the local art college to learn engraving, following in his father's footsteps. It was there that he discovered a tutor named L'Eplattenier. The tutor, for his part, discovered a genius named Jeanneret. In consequence L'Eplattenier shared his passion for the great artists of the past with his prodigious pupil; it was he, if it was anyone, who opened the door and let Jeanneret out. At fifteen Jeanneret won the Diploma of Honour – an international prize – at Turin with a design for a pocket watch, and it was an astonishing piece of work (*see Plate 6*). Chased in silver and gold, the back was a study in balance between the forms of nature, displayed by a bee on some petals of flowers, and those of man, displayed by a cubist pattern of interlocking rectangular shapes. Already this design suggests that an interest in building was getting the upper hand. You have to pinch yourself to believe that this watch is real: the date is 1902 and Jeanneret was not at an art school in Paris – he was at a local college in a narrow Swiss town that was famous for clock making: his only lifeline was L'Eplattenier, and this was with the great masters of the past. Nevertheless, there it is – cubism, abstract art, if you like. Moreover, this beautiful object describes art as it describes the fundamental aims of Le Corbusier's work: perceived in one image is reality, in the other, abstraction; in art neither survives without the existence of the other. Yet the watch was only one of many remarkable works that Jeanneret did at this time. In particular there are his studies from nature, scores of exact paintings of seashells (making mandala forms), leaves and their veins, trees and their structure of branches, and the minutiae of plant life. And then, at seventeen-and-a-half, Jeanneret designed and built his first house – and the client was L'Eplattenier.

Jeanneret had had no architectural training whatever; he

trained himself. Yet what he says about L'Eplattenier's house is, as usual, significant: 'Already I had risked a fool-hardiness in defiance of the wise: two angle windows.' Established rules of convention had to be broken to get to grips with reality. The word 'risked' is particularly interest-ing, for a considerable element of risk underlies everything he did. His next decision meant taking a much bigger risk. The fees he got from L'Eplattenier were spent on his educa-tion – in other words, teaching himself. He decided to travel. It was a risk, but the research had to be done (as Inigo Jones had had to do it) before he could commit him-self as an architect. Until then, until he travelled, Jeanneret must have had very little to go on – only what he had been told by his own acute observation, his parents, and L'Eplat-tenier; he had arrived at a moment when a tradition had ended, and there was no sign of a replacement. He had to understand the past, to know it intimately, before he could begin to consider the present and the future – to create; to do otherwise would mean, in his words, 'wanting to sing when one does not yet have the lungs'. He must have been desperate to get off.

And so Jeanneret left Switzerland for a four-year journey that took him all over Europe and to the Middle East. He went to Budapest, Vienna and Paris, and then to Rumania, Turkey, Czechoslovakia, Serbia and Bulgaria – and he walked. This is surprising, but at least it meant that he saw everything, the detail, the tiny features of existence, slowly, with plenty of time to think. It is not generally known, for instance, that the timber framed houses of Bulgaria and Turkey (part of the international style that stretched across the world in the Middle Ages) with their cantilevered upper storeys, and the volumes these shapes produced set in close juxtaposition, were a great influence in directing his archi-tecture towards the contrast between the horizontal and the vertical space – another theme that remained with him throughout his life. Yet how incredible it seems now, look-ing back from our mobile age, that he should have walked through Europe. When Palladio, for instance, was looking into the classical past he went on horseback, and Inigo Jones, who accompanied earls, presumably travelled by carriage. Jeanneret, however, walked. While there were, of course, trains, there were no cars and no buses. This great walk would seem most odd today. The walk thus establishes an interesting point in history: when Jeanneret set out from Switzerland in 1906 on his long and fantastic career he did so at the very beginning of the machine era that was about to take over the civilization of the twentieth century – fifty years later he would have been blown off the road by the draught from articulated lorries. But then the world was still a quiet, restful place, and there was the time to walk, think and read. There were no aeroplanes and the problems of the environment which Le Corbusier was struggling to solve later on, and which are fast increasing in complexity year by year, were, relatively speaking, non-existent. This should be remembered by those who rush in with criticisms of Le Corbusier's plan of only fifteen years later for a city of three million people. In 1922 nobody had heard of the traffic problem which he foresaw, which is with us now, and to which he was offering a solution then. His city may have been produced too early, but far better this city than ours that have ceased to work because they are jammed with traffic, better than motorways tearing neighbourhoods to shreds, produced too late, or not produced at all.

The walk was Jeanneret's education: and since what he learnt was from personal research, from the observation of his own eyes – and recorded with drawings and notes (seldom a camera, 'a tool for idlers', as Le Corbusier called it) – the knowledge was imprinted on his mind for life. As he says, 'Reality has nothing in common with books of instruction.' And again: 'To draw oneself, to trace the lines handle the volumes, organize the surface ... all this means first to look, and then to observe and finally perhaps to discover ... it is then that inspiration may come.' The dis tinction that he makes between 'looking', 'observing' and 'discovering' demonstrates the accuracy of his thoughts and explanations. 'Inventing, creating, one's whole being is drawn into action,' he goes on. 'Others stood indifferent – but *you* saw!' Yet he treats his walk, a tremendous undertaking, with no fuss; he was a man of action, interested in results, not in the energy expended to achieve them. A great friend, Maurice Jardot, runs through the dates in Le Corbusier's book *My Work* as rapidly as possible, like a film editor cutting rushes. '1907 Budapest, Vienna; in Paris, February 1908. Earned his bread with Auguste Perret ... 1910, retired to the mountains to study technical books on reinforced concrete. 1910 Munich, then Berlin. 1911, off Eastwards, Knapsack on back: Prague, Danube ... Asia Minor. Twenty-one days at Mount Athos. Athens, Acropolis six weeks....' This record, like entries in a diary, represents years of travel and walking. It was fitting that the Parthenon was the climax of his journey. The drawings, however, tell the real story. Look at those drawings Jeanneret made when he was only nineteen or twenty; drawings of places, scale and space, of lakes, mountains, animals, people, buildings. Look at his paintings, done at the same time: they are the paintings of a great artist who had reached maturity without doing thirty years hard labour; that alone makes him a genius. 'It is then that inspiration may come.' Inspiration came to Jeanneret in the Acropolis. His future was there, in its frame of columns. He knew that, when he left.

He was stunned by the Parthenon, as he was by the village architecture of the Greek islands. He called the Parthenon 'a pure creation of the mind' – it is incredible that he could see it so freshly: it might have been built the same year. There was no age barrier: his response was as direct as his observations – what he felt he said, without apology. The temple at the Acropolis was 'the perfect solution', answering 'to a single conception'. It subjected the landscape to the composition, 'so from all sides it is unique.... That

is why no other works of architecture have this grandeur.'
A very different view from Frank Lloyd Wright's – he dis-
liked classical architecture because he said its symmetry
dominated the landscape. Jeanneret was, however, strictly
accurate on this point: the asymmetry of Greek architecture separated it from its Roman counterpart. The
combination of the classical orders in the frame, and its
carefully calculated proportions, and the asymmetry of the
total composition made the balance with the random order
of nature. Here was harmony, and the buildings and the
landscape enlarged each other's magnificence. The symmetry in Roman architecture was stressed by the accen-
tuation of the centre-line, and the Romans, in their
development of the Greek idea, did this to establish a frame
that would help them to arrange their cities and to understand architectural principles. Palladio resolved the conflict
that this symmetry introduced into his own times by scaling
down the importance of the composition and shedding
ornament. Le Corbusier, however, went to the heart of the
matter: he chose to follow the Greeks.

Jeanneret spent six weeks on the Acropolis recording
minute observations in drawings. Like the painter with his
model, he studied the buildings from all possible angles,
noting every subtlety of line, every contour and junction,
every superb curve. After this momentous discovery he
never looked back. But the Greek island architecture was
another important source of inspiration: he was bowled
over by its whitewash. 'Whitewash is absolute', he said,
'Whitewash has been connected with the home of men
since the birth of mankind.' Once more he had been carried
away by a discovery: something that an ordinary mortal
might regard as picturesque, or charming, was for him a
heroic theme of life, an epic. Whitewash, for most of us, is
country cottages, the interior of a kitchen, the walls lining a
lane out of a village on the way to the sea. For Le Corbusier, however, whitewash was 'the wealth of the poor

man and the rich man, of every man, just as bread, milk and water are the wealth of slave and king alike'.

Le Corbusier never failed to convey his sense of wonder, whatever the medium – buildings, writings, drawings; like a child who is seeing everything for the first time, he found the world a marvellous place – the grass, the sky, the sea, the moss, the sticks from the fir trees lying in the snow, the intricate details of a Venetian palace – to him, all these things were amazing, and he conveys this amazement. It was an unclouded freshness and spontaneity which never left him – 'I have never ceased to be a student,' he said when he was just on forty and had completed the Villa Savoye. In his sixties, he said of the gap of light between the walls and the roof at the chapel at Ronchamp : 'It will amaze.' And, a little later, on a Monitor programme for BBC television he said : 'I am a young man of seventy'. But in the Greek islands he had seen whitewash as a bond between people. 'To observe and finally perhaps to discover ... it is then that inspiration may come.' Again, inspiration did come : whitewash was also a bond between the buildings of the island villages. This bond was on a visual level; like the bare essentials that hold people together, whitewash was a bond that held aesthetics together, so that any combination of shapes, sizes and objects – walls, houses, churches, bell-towers – was possible provided that the whole picture was white. Above all, he fell in love with the purity of white; his ambition was to purify architecture, just as Wittgenstein's ambition was to purify language, Schönberg's to purify music, and Eliot's to purify poetry. Thus white became the bond between Le Corbusier's early buildings. In consequence, it became the bond between all the European architectural modern movements of the 1920s and 1930s : white was the theme that held the total picture together.

The use of whitewash as a main theme in an architecture where all elements were totally unexpected and original was another of Le Corbusier's inventions; it was for this reason, as much as any other, that he became the leader of modern European architecture. In a sense, this theme recalls the watch he designed when he was fifteen, chased in silver, steel, copper and gold. In this there are many materials within a tiny area, and to get a bit of extra sparkle he added some jewels as well. But the design succeeded because he made a frame; or, to put it another way, exploited a frame that already existed. Within the circle of the watch two shapes of a quite different character clearly interlock, resembling the ancient eastern symbol of the mandala. These shapes, when combined, describe balance as the mandala describes balance; which is apposite, since the interlocking cogs that make a watch work operate on the principle of balance. However, the subject matter of the two halves of the design – man's order (represented by the formal jigsaw) and nature's freedom (represented by the bee fertilizing the flowers) – conjures up the picture of a scientist examining an interesting specimen under a microscope : in this case, the artist examining architecture – its complicated details crystallized as a pattern on the back of a watch. Here was a microscosm : in this tiny picture he saw how things could be free. But, like architecture, the pattern operates on a number of levels. On one, it is a pattern and nothing more; on another, it shows that order leads to freedom, and that the design reflects the workings of the object which it ornaments; on yet another, the frame accepts various different materials. As in life Le Corbusier's work was inspired by such forces : the aim was to close the gap between man and nature, and this aim has its embryonic beginnings in the design of the watch.

The whitewash of the Greek island architecture helps to clarify the idea. If the irregular foreground of a village, with the whiteness of its various forms, is set against the freedom of the countryside, it makes a picture which approximates to the composition on the back of the watch – the jigsaw of plain interlocking shapes, like the whitewash, frames its counterpart in the intricate web of nature. At the same time, however, it has to be remembered that Jean-neret designed the watch before he went to the Greek islands and, of course, before he had seen the Parthenon. This seems to disclose his genius. It shows that when he went off on his enormous walk he knew what he was looking for, and he found it at the Parthenon and in the Greek islands. The mind of the artist becomes clearer. Jeanneret's genius was mature when he was fifteen, but what it needed, and needed quickly, was experience. Just as the earth, spinning in space, attracts an atmosphere by gravity, so the artist, acting like a magnet, draws the material he needs to himself, and this surrounds him like an atmosphere. Perhaps what Jeanneret needed then, back in 1910, was a clear lead, and the confirmation of his own ideas; hence the walk, and the tremendous labour of stock-piling information. The past supplied the experience he required; he found order and harmony at the Parthenon, and a colour in the islands. The next step seems to have been the experiment with cubes in his project for the *Ateliers d'Artistes (see Plate 3)*. This experiment answered, as Le Corbusier would have said, 'to a single conception'. From all sides it was unique.

The influence of ancient Greek principles is plain in these drawings. Nevertheless, the fact remains that this design dates from 1910 and, like the watch, before the records say he actually visited the Parthenon. This suggests what the watch suggests: that he saw solutions, immediately, as artists do see solutions with mysteriously little help, grasping ideas that are in the air: the Parthenon was like the discovery of a god who enlarged his experience and confirmed he was on the right lines. Of course, when he designed the *Ateliers d'Artistes*, he must have had some knowledge of the architecture of ancient Greece, and the conception for the artists' studios shows how quickly he soaked up all available material around him. The disciplines that he followed in the design stretch back two thousand years, and it was from these that, three decades later, he invented the Modulor, a system of measurements for relating the proportion of buildings to the proportion of people: the Modulor was really a highly complex development of the ancient Greek diagram (*see Plate 17*). What the Greeks had noticed was that when a man stood with his arms outstretched and his legs apart, his hands and feet described that most perfect and simple shape, the circle; the centre point for this was the navel. From the circle the Greeks arrived at the square drawn within the circle, and in Leonardo's and Dürer's diagrams the corners of this square are pegged out by the figure's hands and feet. This shape had a more common usage than the circle, but both forms became the basis of the Greeks' theory of architectural design: since a building cannot be related to a man by size it must be related by proportion. This diagram could then be divided up on the centre-line of the navel both vertically and horizontally, so making semi-circles, squares within the square and, with the addition of diagonals, triangles. As with the Modulor, a range of measures results, all of which, derived from the circle and the square, are directly related to the proportion of the human figure. And this range was then used as a means for calculating the size of façades, volumes, doors and other openings. It created an aesthetic system of parts that influenced the proportion of the western architectural tradition (as indeed the six foot by three foot mat – the 'Tatami' – ordered the architectural proportion of the Japanese tradition) from the Greek temple to the Corbusier Centre in Zurich.

In *Towards a New Architecture* Le Corbusier discusses the method of the Greeks, and describes their principles of design as the 'regulating lines'. But he knew all about their methods years before when he was at work on the *Ateliers d'Artistes*: here was the square (the plan), the cube (the artists' studios – the square projected in three dimensions), the triangle (the pyramidal meeting room at the centre). Diagrammatically, Le Corbusier crystallized the classical conception as a square derived from the cube, with a square piece taken out in the middle to form a peristyle. Now at

1 Villa Savoye at Poissy, designed and built between 1929 and 1931

2 *The Zebra and the Parachute* by Christopher Wood: the sun-terrace at Villa Savoye

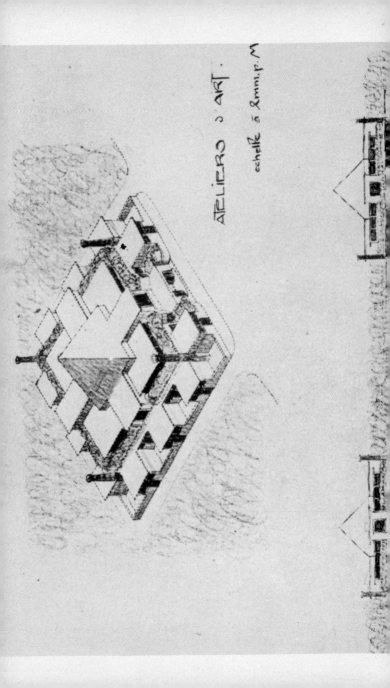

ATELIERS D'ART.

echelle à 2mm.p.M

3 *Opposite*: Le Corbusier's drawing for the
  Ateliers d'Artistes, 1910
4 *Above*: The Chapel of Notre Dame du Haut at Ronchamp
  as it appears over the hill
5 One of Le Corbusier's early drawings of the Chapel at Ronchamp

6 The Watch, winner of the diploma at the
International Exhibition of the Decorative Arts in Turin, 1902

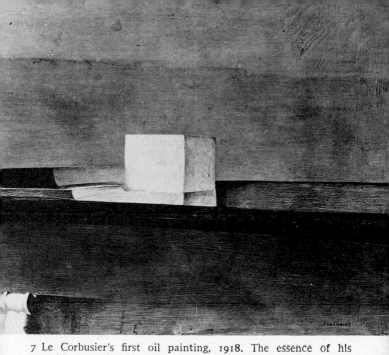

7 Le Corbusier's first oil painting, 1918. The essence of his architecture shows in this painting – the play between the curve and the cube

8 Villa la Roche, 1923

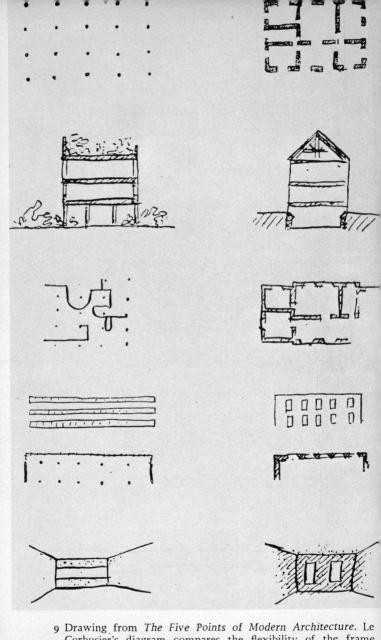

9 Drawing from *The Five Points of Modern Architecture*. Le Corbusier's diagram compares the flexibility of the frame structure (left) with the limitations of traditional methods (right)

10 The sun-deck at the Duval factory at Sainte-Dié, built between 1946 and 1951

11 Plan of Algiers, 1930

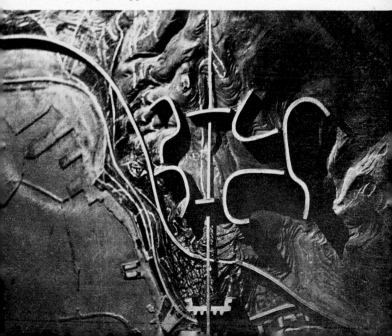

12 *Pavillon Suisse* in the *cité universitaire* at Paris, 1931

this point you notice the likeness to the watch again. The outline of this composition was, of course, the circle and not the square. But when a piece of this circle is taken away the form of the design is discovered; and a harmony is revealed between what you could call the order of the rectangles and the disorder of nature, between common-sense and the imagination – a harmony that is fundamental to the making of all art. In the *Ateliers d'Artistes* the aesthetic aims are the same as are the means employed; and, in principle, these aims display the essence of the classical method – the square at the centre subtracted to reveal the form. In the watch, the two pieces of the composition are parts of a circle: at the studios, the peripheral buildings, the spaces or courtyards between them, the pyramidal centre and the square outline of the total composition are really all part of a much larger discipline – the cube, the upper half of which has been removed, leaving behind an ingenious yet simple arrangement of studios round a meeting space. Jeanneret had brought light into the centre of the cube, and all that was left of it was the outline of the square plan that regulated the interior composition. The *Ateliers d'Artistes* was a three-dimensional development of the relief on the pocket watch, and thus a considerable step forward. Although the designs were, in principle, alike, Jeanneret had taken the idea of the watch into the area of architecture: at the *Ateliers d'Artistes* he had accomplished that essential harmony between commonsense and the imagination, between a community on the one hand, and an aesthetic order for the whole on the other.

The themes of these two compositions, seen together, provide a map of his work. It is the parts of a building that Le Corbusier left out that are, in every case, so singularly interesting. The subtraction of some piece of the cube meant entry of light; and the entry of light meant the creation of form. Now this connects with the contemporary cubist movement in painting, the vision of which was shared by Le Corbusier. On the one hand he said that 'architecture is in the telephone instrument and in the Parthenon'; but he cannot be separated from the last wave of the Impressionist movement – Cézanne, Matisse, Gris, Derain, Braque and Picasso – any more than he can be separated from mechanization and engineering. By the time the *Ateliers d'Artistes* was conceived, Picasso and Braque were already deeply involved in cubist experiments. Braque had just completed a series of pictures of L'Estaque, and one of these, called *Houses at L'Estaque*, painted in 1908, has a remarkable affinity with the *Ateliers d'Artistes* in its forms, and the separation of the forms : in the use of the cube, the pyramid (the points of roof pitches and gable ends), the foliage filling the gaps between walls (the planes); and in the discovery of a harmony of the ordered geometry of man with the soft roundness and freedom of nature. There is a likeness, too, between the relief on the back of the pocket watch and this picture. The relief appears to have evolved from drawings Jeanneret did of plants among rocks. In the painting Braque sees the houses as rocks among foliage. Both artists were, therefore, doing the same kind of thing – giving nature an order through the means of cubism. But, more important perhaps, the watch, the painting and the studios show how closely shared was the vision of Jeanneret and Braque. It was with painters like him – and like Cézanne, Picasso – that Le Corbusier's name will always be most closely linked, and not with contemporaries like Adolf Loos (who introduced him to reinforced concrete), or Peter Behrens (for whom he worked for a time), or Walter Gropius and Mies van der Rohe whom he met in Behrens' studio; or with Horta, Berlager and Mackintosh whose sculptural work of the 1900s certainly influenced him, and which he came across, again, when he was with Behrens. Le Corbusier came to architecture through painting, and he stepped off from the Parthenon (*see Plate* 7). He was part of a fantastically brilliant family of artists in which his immediate relatives were Braque, Picasso, Léger and Gris; at the head of it was undoubtedly Cézanne.

Unlike a brother, more like a cousin, Le Corbusier seldom met the painter bit of the family : he probably knew Léger best. Yet he talked the same language as the Cubists and his comments on space, light, colour and form are often scarcely distinguishable from remarks made by Cézanne. The word 'light', inherited from the Impressionists, was particularly high on the list; so were words like 'planes', 'perspective', 'structure', 'sculpture' and 'nature'. Cézanne, who wrote with the same accuracy and attention to detail and vigour as Le Corbusier, puts the aims of painting most clearly : 'It is in the modelling that one draws ... one detaches things from their environment – the daylight alone gives the body its appearance.' Talking of light, he says : 'There are no lines, no forms, only contrasts.' And he told a friend that if he wanted to understand the meaning of nature better he should try to see it in 'the cylinder, the sphere, the cone, putting everything in proper perspective so that each side of an object or plane is directed towards a central point. Lines parallel to the horizon give breadth, that is, a section of Nature.... Lines perpendicular to the horizon give depth....' Ozenfant made this point, too, and so did Georg Schmidt.

Le Corbusier said much the same thing : 'The great problems of modern building will be worked out in geometry. ... Our eyes are made to see forms in light; shades and brightness reveal forms; cubes, cones, cylinders or pyramids are the great forms that light reveals well.... It is because of this that they are beautiful forms, the most beautiful forms.' The geometric connection between the *Pigeon Tower at L'Estaque* and the light shafts at Ronchamp is immediately clear. Cézanne then says : 'Light is a thing that cannot be reproduced but must be represented by something else, colour....' Parallels, verticals, horizontals, the discovery of light through colour – these were Cézanne's 'regulating lines'. Sometimes it seems that Le Corbusier, through his medium, was nearer to the whole being of Cézanne's art than anybody else. 'The architectural elements,'

Le Corbusier said of the Law Courts at Chandigarh, 'are light and shadow, the wall and space' – in other words, as Cézanne says, 'contrasts'. The objectives of the two artists were very alike; different problems but similar ends, as indicated by Cézanne's remark that 'each side of an object or plane is directed towards a central point'. Both artists' work had the drive, focus and concentration that this remark implies. Le Corbusier put this view rather differently : 'The plan is the generator … without a plan there is disorder, arbitrariness.' From the plan, the architecture radiated outwards, the reverse of Cézanne's direction 'towards a central point'. Both artists derived their inspiration from classical foundations of order in structure and proportion, and both maintained that this order must be held exactly in focus until the end – the very end. And both believed that this could only be accomplished by immense dedication and energy, by, Le Corbusier said, 'modesty, continuity, perseverence'.

The spaces in Cézanne's early pictures were arranged with infinite care and patience – the *Fishing Village at L'Estaque*, for instance, or *Madame Cézanne with the bent head* (this took five years to complete) of the 1870s; and the verticals and horizontals of the *Mennesy Bridge* were stressed with the firmness of the Villa Savoye – in both cases, these were the groundwork for schemes of genius to come. For the verticals and horizontals, the cylinders and cones which possessed both artists, were displayed, as time went on, more and more by 'contrasts' and by 'light and shadow', less and less by lines. In Cézanne's later paintings and watercolours it is the accurate placing of colour that reveals the structure of a face or the strength of Ste Victoire; similarly, in Le Corbusier's late buildings – La Tourette, the Chapel at Ronchamp, the buildings at Chandigarh – it is light and shadow that describes the contours of volumes within, or emphasizes the shelter and its supports. Le Corbusier, like Cézanne, had boiled his art down to the bones; all effects were achieved by the simplest means. The hard form, so necessary at the Villa Stein, had vanished away, for it was no longer necessary to the realization of Le Corbusier's conception of the 'perfect solution'.

Le Corbusier, however, had to understand the hard facts of the classical disciplines before he could begin to relinquish them, in the same way that he had to grasp the possibilities of the machine before he could begin to reject its aesthetic. Because the comprehension of both happened more or less simultaneously, the spirit of both go hand-in-hand in his early buildings and paintings; they point to one end – the world about him. And so Le Corbusier began work on the cube. His material was reinforced concrete. The limits of the form, and the material, established the frame within which to work. He was like a sculptor with a block of pure white stone in front of him, and a hammer and chisel in his hands. He said that it was by 'the channel of my painting that I came to architecture'; and, on another occasion, 'paintings were painted ... which were potential sculpture. . . .' Like a sculptor, he wanted to discover what mysteries lay inside the block of stone, what shapes and spaces could be revealed by the cutting away of unnecessary bits. But unlike Epstein, for instance, whose courage and sensitivity dug out arms and legs from a hard slab, Le Corbusier was finding spaces for living – corridors, kitchens, bathrooms, terraces. Looked at like this, the dividing line between architecture and sculpture does indeed seem negligible. Epstein opened up the slab and, in doing so, brought light to the limbs he made: light and shadow described the forms. Le Corbusier opened up the cube and brought light to the volumes within – it is light that reveals circular staircases and curved screens; hence his insistence on shape. In a sense, these voluptuous and relaxed connections between one part of a house and another suggest the figure of a woman – the ramps are like outstretched muscles. Thus the forms discovered in the cube could be as descriptive of the character of a human being as the relationships of proportion measured by the Greek diagram. This explains, too, the likeness between the appearance of La Tourette and the standing figure by Picasso. The kind of things that Le Corbusier found in the cube are as much a part of human beings as the forms Picasso invented to describe a nose, or the pipe in the mouth of a Cézanne man. Le Corbusier put the matter simply: 'The plan proceeds from within outward'.

Le Corbusier wrote that the happiness he had found in design existed for others who were as determined as he to search for it. The forms and volumes he found in the cube – and those that he had not found – were also, he would have doubtless claimed, as universally available as happiness. For one could assume, for the sake of argument, that a cube consists of millions of diagonal lines, or cylinders, or blocks, or some other geometric shape. If a triangle, for instance, of the diagonal lines of a certain depth was then removed a volume would be left which has one corner that is a right-angle and one side that makes a diagonal across the cube: a sleeping balcony in a studio, maybe. If, on the other hand, the cube is seen to be composed of hundreds of small blocks, an area of these could be removed leaving behind a square volume in the cube: the enclosed garden terraces on the top floor of the *Pavillon Suisse* in Paris, for example. Again, it could be said that any kind of curve or circle exists in a solid, and that when the adjoining part is removed these curves or circles are then revealed: the staircase at the Villa Savoye. But, at the same time, it could be said that by this means he was also emphasizing the outline of the cube which contained these shapes or objects; and that, in consequence, the space between the cylinder – or the triangular balcony, or a square object – and the outline of the cube gain importance. But then, having subtracted a quantity of material to make spaces round staircases, boiler flues, and columns; and having, by this means, stressed the real value of the frame, he begins another process – the addition of new parts: not merely the cupboards, the hand-rails, screens and so on, but, much more important, the parts brought by people – their taste, sense of colour, furniture and the rest of human trivia. It is people who must complete the unfinished work. Le Corbusier left his buildings unfinished for others to fill in with their detail. He designed, if you like, a background for living, in the same way that classical architecture, with its manifestations in the community frame of Georgian architecture, provided a background order that not merely accepted, but encouraged, the contribution of others.

The discipline which held the various shapes and other happenings inside together was the outline of the cube, or derivations of the cube. This had to remain in control if freedom of form could exist elsewhere: the frame of a building or buildings is like the laws that govern society – without these laws there is anarchy, and without the frame there is visual anarchy. At the *Pavillon Suisse*, for instance, the frame is a long block of bedrooms supported on a single line of columns, and this accepts the variations in the sweeping lines of the hall and common room beneath it. On a roof terrace that Le Corbusier designed overlooking the Champs Elysées he suggests a frame with objects that stand about within the space, and outside it – the presence of the Arc de Triomphe poking up from the avenue below is as important to the design as the fireplace (a surrealist touch from Magritte which echoes the shape of the Arc), some walls, steps and other objects: all protect the space as a screen shelters an exposed place. Le Corbusier stresses this point – 'a space must be comfortable', he says. To be physically comfortable it must also be aesthetically comfortable. The frame of architecture provides this comfort, whether you are sitting on the sun terrace at the Villa Savoye or in the garden of a Georgian square. And, again, once this frame is established, the contribution of others can begin. By stressing the fact that a comprehensible diagram was central to the continuity of architectural evolution Le Corbusier was, at the same time, calling attention to the individual by giving him an external order that diminishes the effect of human muddle.

At the *Dom-ino* house, which Le Corbusier designed in 1913, he was thinking along the same lines. It was a project for rebuilding, quickly and cheaply, towns that had been devastated by the war. What he invented was a structural system (the first example of an industrialized method of system building with prefabricated parts ever to be designed) that was independent of the functions of the plan of the house. It was to be made of standard elements that could be fitted together, as he said, thus 'permitting a great diversity in the grouping of the houses.... It then remained to fit up a home inside the frame.' This design, therefore, forecast modern industrial building techniques, which, thoroughly commercialized, are universally accepted today. But the aesthetic of the cube, discovered in the *Ateliers d'Artistes*, remained. The floors and roof maintain its outline in the plan view, and the columns maintain it in the section. And so, whatever the situation – whether it was to meet the destruction of a war or to give his parents a house on Lake Geneva – the architecture of a building was tied to the cube. Architecture was sculpture, but sculpture through which you walk. The Chapel at Ronchamp is a place for prayer but it is also an enormous white shape. A balcony inside the Villa Stein at Garches was a balcony for sitting about on, but it was also a rectangular, fresh, white form which sparkled with vitality in a double storey volume. The flowing white screens on the roof of the Villa Savoye give protection from the wind but they are also sculpture. In the early work – the work of the 1920s – Le Corbusier extracted all the geometric sculpture he could out of the cube, carrying the sharp white form of the outside inside, so that the whole – the exterior and the interior – were conceived as one. He did this by winning the battle for space on which architecture of any time, and in any place in the world, has always depended for its existence. But the ways in which he interpreted space, and described it, were entirely new and original, and brought the presence of the cube and its frame into vivid prominence in the process (*see Plate* 9). It is no wonder that his white style spread everywhere – to Holland, Switzerland, Germany and, finally, to England.

It was with Le Corbusier's struggle for space, and his resolve to counter all problems arising out of the cube and its contents, that another complex theme introduced itself; namely, the possibility of being able to sense – if not entirely to see – a building from every point, whether inside or outside, or both. This theme brought his ideas into the fourth-dimensional sphere which was, at that time, being studied by artists like Picasso and Braque. The opening in the curved façade at the Villa La Roche, together with the open space beneath it, reveals the shape and depth of the entire object at a single glance (*see Plate* 7). And at some small workmen's cottages that he designed a year later, in 1924, he divided the cube into two spaces with a diagonal that made a triangular sleeping balcony, transforming a small space into a large one – the whole length of the cottage was used, as well as its total height. This recalls Cézanne, too, when he talked about horizontal and perpendicular lines and planes and was suggesting ways in which the complex order of nature could be transferred to a canvas in terms of structure. By digging out his spaces from the interior of the cube, Le Corbusier was doing much the same thing – but transferring the structure of materials to man. He shows us this structure: states it and restates it. At Pessac, a low cost housing scheme near Bordeaux of 1925, the more rambling plan of La Roche contracts to a cube, and a combination of cubes is arranged to make a variety of housing forms. The outline of this cube appears on the roof as a mere concrete skeleton that outlines the shape with a flat top; this skeleton is repeated over a number of roofs in line, giving, once more, a curious illusion of space through continuity and distance – like reflections of a single image in face-to-face mirrors. But the frame of the whole is the cube, and the insistent repetition of cubes stresses the importance of this frame. The open roof garden draws it to the attention: the outline of the structure is completed, drawing attention to the overall shape.

Le Corbusier attempted the form again in 1926, this time at Maison Cook, one of a number of houses he built in and around Paris in the 1920s. Again the square plan is adopted, but now the interior curves of non-structural walls are more pronounced than they were at, for example, the Villa La Roche. Again he opens up the cube to make a roof garden, but now he subtracts the ground floor too – all that is left of it is an entrance hall and a single column. No sooner had he set up the cube as a discipline than he began to break it down to bare aesthetic essentials, bringing the purity of the white cube out into the foreground at its sharpest and most sculptural. Le Corbusier was a down-to-earth man, a realist at all times. For him, the cube was an aesthetic tool to give order and pleasure: it was not allowed to take over the design, it was there to do a job. At Maison Cook – as at Pessac, as at the Villas Stein and Savoye – it enabled him to carry through his discovery of a roof as a garden. He wanted every part of his buildings to be used, known intimately and enjoyed. The subtraction of the ground floor meant ease of entry, yet it also meant that the underside of the structure could be seen – the inside became part of the outside. And the introduction of the roof garden (*see Plate 10*) at the top meant that the building opened out into the sun and light with a private view of the sky that was unique to that building. Le Corbusier had first worked on this idea in his 'green' city project of 1922 when he brought the garden into the heart of his blocks of flats. But at Pessac, Maison Cook and the rest, the invention led on to much bigger things – the roof gardens of the apartment buildings in Geneva and Paris, and of the *Pavillon Suisse*, the Salvation Army hostel, the *Unités*, the Secretariat in Chandigarh, the monastery of La Tourette, the Corbusier Centre in Zurich. The roof garden was another life's theme; they were real gardens with long grass and trees, paving and furniture, and, although high up above towns and landscape, they possessed a solidity that one finds down on the ground. At the Villa Stein, in the Paris surburb of Garches, he took the roof garden a step further; it is larger, more expansive and generous than Maison Cook's. Here he is at work on the cube again, this time turning closer attention to the interior volumes. Behind the flat façades with their long horizontal windows undulating shapes appear; the combination of the cube and the curve – again a theme which was central to all his work – recalls his first oil painting of 1918 (*see Plate 8*); the curved walls to corridors, the circular ends to stairs and the rounded corners become the modelling that stands inside the familiar shell. Up on the familiar sun-terrace, the cylindrical forms evaporate, are described in the air with handrails. Once more the objects standing about in space are freed by the presence of the frame – shape detaches them, as Cézanne said, 'from their environment'.

The Villa Stein was completed in 1927. A year later at a house in Carthage he is still working on the cube and its ramifications, but here, because of the much hotter climate, he turned from the modelling of forms in the enclosed interior to the modelling of the section of the building: curves vanish, walls are straight, corners square – the rejection of the softness of curves seem to reflect the ruthless hard glare of the sun. The variations that Le Corbusier discovered in the cube are now shown in vertical, interlocking spaces – as balconies which float over each other on alternate floors – the first evidence of the *brise soleil* of the *L'Unité d'Habitation* at Marseilles of twenty years later. Again, faithful to the climate, this house had a much more open structure than anything he had done before. He wanted the breezes to drift through and cool the interior – hence the openness of the volumes – and this, too, suggests work that he did after the war, this time in India, at Chandigarh. Then, in the following year, came his last work with the cube and whitewash, at least for a time, the Villa Savoye.

For Le Corbusier, this was 'the perfect solution' – it was unique on all four sides. But the design was inspired from another direction too: the house is placed on a mound in the centre of a bare field, so that, from the first floor, Le Corbusier said, the four horizons could be seen. This conception recalls the Villa Capra by Palladio with its plan of ten squares forming a cross, and the four porticos that completed the cross in three dimensions commanded the magnificent view from all four façades. At the Villa Savoye Le Corbusier takes this idea further. The horizontal windows are continuous and therefore the view is continuous. Then parts of the interior are subtracted to make the sun-terrace on the first floor, and this means that there is also a view from the centre of the house which includes the sky. Le Corbusier had broken the cube down with such vigour that only the parallel bands of whitewashed concrete of the central floor remain as a frame for the complexities and curves of the interior plan. Yet the Villa preserves throughout strong links with the classical past, at least in spirit. For is it not possible to see, in fact, the Piazza Navona in the Villa Savoye – the open ground floor with the café life of awnings and tables spilling out on to the pavements, the central floors conveying a calm which gives order to the square, and the cottage architecture which clambers like creepers over the roof-tops? The truth is really quite simple. By keeping faith with the same laws which governed classical architecture, Le Corbusier recalls such associations as the Piazza Navona, and catches the spirit of the classical idea in one dazzling glimpse crystallizing this idea with a single image of his own. For here is the open ground floor with the house spilling into the field, here is the central floor spreading an air of great calm over the whole composition, and here is life climbing out of it into the sunlight of the terrace, and on to the roof with ramps and flowing white screens. On one level, you are shown the object in space, the spirit of the Parthenon and the frame of columns between which everything happens; on another level, the Villa Savoye suggests the spirit of seventeenth-century Rome. Le Corbusier was a poet, for only a poet can condense so much into so little.

You look again. The Villa Savoye is, after all, just a house, as a figure by Michelangelo is a likeness of a man, and a painting by Cézanne is a picture of a bridge with a river running beneath it: familiar rooms, familiar hands and feet, familiar leaves on trees and blades of grass. Then the process of involvement with the architecture begins once more. The workings of the house are neatly stored on the ground floor, out of the way – the heating system, a garage, a staff flat; all this so ingeniously solved that you feel that Le Corbusier was methodically and consciously laying the foundations for an idea of genius. On the sun-terrace above you are suddenly confronted with the white sculpture of the architecture again, and the presence of its maker: you can feel the hand that made the triangular form which is the ramp, and the concrete slab which is the table, and the white screens above you coiling round like a shell; he sculpted the enormous basin in the bathroom and cast the chaise-longue at the end of the bath. You are in the sculpture, in the monastic whiteness of the block of stone that he excavated and shaped, the interior of which, a moment ago, you saw from below, in the field. For little remains of the cube: Le Corbusier opened the façades like the back of a watch and revealed the works: inside and outside sculpture are one: and the fourth dimension enters the picture as a means of observing the complete object from the sides, from the inside or the outside.

At the Villa Savoye he achieved what he set out to do with the cube, and had started working on long before at the *Ateliers d'Artistes* in 1910. In this house he brings together every source of inspiration and experience available to him at that time: the past with all its ramifications; the classical frame and the diagram of proportion, the memory of whitewash from the Greek islands; and the vigorous imagery of modern technology. No wonder Christopher Wood was inspired, no wonder the Villa carried off the imaginations of architects all over Europe; no wonder the self-appointed ambassadors of Le Corbusier – architects like Chemayeff, Breuer, Neutra, Rietveld, Lubetkin and Wells Coates – transported his ideas to America, Switzerland, Holland, England and elsewhere. This strange object in a field became the romantic dream upon which the whole modern architectural movement centred.

The Villa Savoye says something else, quite bluntly.

It held out a dream for a better future. But it was a fragile one in the twentieth century world, for the Villa again demonstrates that everything Le Corbusier made was unique to, and inseparable from the situation in which it found itself, and so was dependent on its surroundings remaining unchanged – a bad gamble today. In the case of the Villa Savoye, the house was designed for a meadow that was joined to the village of Poissy by a track, around which there were trees and empty fields. The whiteness and openness of the house made a single statement of great force in this emptiness; it reproduced the space of the surroundings in the interior, of which the exterior was a candid expression.

This statement has disappeared, for good. In the years following the war a masterpiece of the imagination was allowed to decay. The house was used by the Nazis as a headquarters and, passing through their brutal hands, the whole point of the building was lost. After they left, the Savoyes gave up all idea of living there, and sold it to the Poissy authorities. It remained empty; it was used for storing hay, and birds nested in it; and it was eventually saved from demolition by the sudden intervention of André Malraux at the time of Le Corbusier's death. He saw that the house was restored. In the meantime, however, the suburbs of Paris had swarmed in like mad invaders. Poissy was swallowed up by post-war industrial chaos – the Simca factories and the office blocks with their usual side-effects of shopping centres, supermarkets, housing estates, highway plans, suburban chalets, tree-felling and the rest: the track became a road and a tarmac car-park, and a vast and hideous school was built in the field next to the villa. The picture was in pieces: the romantic dream was gone.

Now the house is imprisoned by the town and the school peers in with gaoler's eyes. Every room is watched. You are surrounded, persecuted by all that a house should protect you from – great numbers of unknown people. The meadow which the sundeck and the relaxed and spacious plan were meant to reflect has been taken away; and so, with extraordinary clarity, you see that architecture exists not only within itself but also within the setting for which it has been specially made. The house and the meadow belonged to each other, and needed each other, like lovers. The soft grass, the quiet, the trees were as essential to the house as the smell of white hawthorn and the sound of a tinkling bell and the lilac are to recollections of Proust and M. Swann at Illiers. The Villa Savoye was meant to be in the country. It hates the school: they are old enemies – one of art, the other of all that is shoddy and ugly. The school is the familiar aesthetic outrage but here, in a way perhaps to be expected with Le Corbusier, there is a special twist. In normal circumstances it is some old building that is violated by a contemporary development, and to an extent, therefore, one is able to remain uninvolved. But in this case the whole cycle of events was accomplished within forty years, and the horror is so much nearer and much more violent because the target of attack is part of one's own background.

Thus it becomes clear that a building by Le Corbusier – as unique, as precious as any great work of art of any time – is vulnerable to destruction in a way that a painting, say, is not: a building cannot be moved unless it is, like the Corbusier Centre at Zurich, demountable. For a start, the weekend house he built outside Paris has been demolished. But the Chapel at Ronchamp is not entirely safe because it is on a hill, the *L'Unité d'Habitation* at Marseilles has already vanished behind tower blocks, so losing its lifelines with the space of the sea and the mountains; La Tourette on its grass slope has, to one's horror, been converted into some kind of conference centre, and the step is short to swimming pools, bars, motels, hotels, restaurants, sticking to its edges like scum. And, at a stroke, the exquisite pleasure conveyed by such buildings disappears; and their meaning as architecture, as a description of a place and its atmosphere, is totally obscured.

A freedom had emerged in the Villa Savoye which showed itself in different ways in small houses later on in the 1930s when Le Corbusier began to shed the classical disciplines. This freedom also shows in his paintings and drawings. Having got to grips with Greece and modern mechanization simultaneously, he began to relinquish them, to loosen their hold on his ideas. The drawings of grasses and bottles, and of cylinders, cubes and cones of the early 1920s were, rather like Léger's, put together with such precision that the shapes of the various objects interlock like wheels in a machine. But the drawings he was doing a few years afterwards (the sketch of an important rock outside Marseilles in 1927, and the study 'With a Box of Matches') drop all associations with this kind of imagery. And in the paintings of the mid-1930s, the shapes flowed away into the lovely voluptuous lines of women's bodies. It is difficult to see any influences from contemporaries like Picasso and Braque. Le Corbusier's only source of inspiration was what he saw through his own eyes: natural phenomena: pebbles, bones, rocks; 'objects like these,' he said, 'are spread before us, look at them and ... you will then have a storehouse of inspiration to draw upon....'

In the 1930s Le Corbusier was simultaneously active in several different media. His drawings were like research notes of ideas perceived in the world about him, records for the 'storehouse' of particular observations that would someday lead to something of importance: the ear of *Josephine*, drawn in 1929, is extremely interesting. At the same time he was painting – he called it 'a terrible, intense, pitiless battle, without witnesses, a duel between the artist and himself.'

He was designing furniture, in particular two armchairs, a tubular steel chair and a *chaise-longue*, all of which are being produced today as 'status' objects for the wealthy and sold for very high prices; as examples of modern furniture, they have never been surpassed. He was writing – in 1929 alone he completed a vast number of essays, packed with information. These dealt with the principles of modern house design and the fundamentals of town planning, and included illustrations and diagrams of anything from traffic communication to studies of cupboards and ways of arranging clothes on hangers. These were originally written for *L'Esprit Nouveau* and they were republished as *Précisions* in 1960, a book partly financed by Le Corbusier to keep the price down for students. At the same time he was also designing town plans for Anvers, Algiers (*see Plate 11*), Antwerp and Brazil, the vast and immensely complex Palace of the Soviets (1931 – for Moscow but not built), and the series of blocks of flats he conceived for Algiers in the form of steps; these may be regarded as the prototype for the fashion in 'stepped' housing that spread across in England in the 1960s, losing sight of Le Corbusier's initial idea on the way. But, in addition to all these projects, Le Corbusier was dazzling the world with buildings like the red stone and sheer glass of an office block in Moscow, a hostel for the Salvation Army and the *Pavillon Suisse* in the *cité universitaire* (both in Paris), flats in Geneva and overlooking the Bois du Boulogne, and the Education building in Rio. Although the works in Moscow, Geneva and Paris were designed at roughly the same time as the Villa Savoye was completed (the flats were conceived a year or two later), he had dropped concrete as the predominant material and had gone over to steel and glass. At the *Pavillon Suisse*, completed only a year after the Villa, all that was left of the earlier period were the columns which lifted the main structure off the ground (*See Plate 12*). On this occasion, however, the break was total : here was a single conception where the glass façade, derived from a repetition of five squares, was entirely free from the ground. In almost all his buildings Le Corbusier succeeded in breaking down the barrier between the interior and the exterior; at Maison Cook, the Villa Savoye, the monastery of La Tourette and the Palace of Justice at Chandigarh, the outside is allowed to melt into the inside, and the abruptness of entry is removed. At Maison Cook the open ground floor is already part of the hall; at the Palace of Justice the enormous coloured supports to the canopy are the connection betweeen the vastness of India outside and the reduction in the scale of the interior beyond them. Palladio put the matter simply when he said that the 'portico pointed out the entrance'. The removal of barriers at Maison Cook and the Palace of Justice does precisely this – openness draws us in. At the *Pavillon Suisse* Le Corbusier leaves it to the columns to direct us. In fact, the plan is like a conjuring trick : to reach the upper floors, you have to go into a separate part where the common room is, returning to the main building by way of a staircase, having taken in a curved wall (derived from the snow laden bough of the fir) and a mural by the architect on the journey. At the same time, his grip on twentieth-century technology was complete : he saw it as a tool, as a sculptor sees a chisel, as a means to an architectural end : now he was in his early forties he had mastered his craft. Such things as the integration of the steel superstructure and the organization of services like heating, of sliding windows and hidden blinds were perfectly achieved : today, over forty years later, it would be hard – if not impossible – to find much outside his own work that equals the superb details of the *Pavillon Suisse*. Le Corbusier was in complete command, demonstrating that all our architectural problems can be solved when the right means are used in the right way.

This building was a break-through, and gave modern architecture a shove forward. At the same time he was designing the hostel for the Salvation Army. He was commissioned to do this after he had fitted out some houseboats for tramps in the 1920s – these boats, painted black and white and one of the first works he did in Paris, are still on the Seine. At the hostel, the glass façade withdrew to become a neutral background of complete simplicity – a background in front of which others could perform, in this case, the delicate interplay of cube and cylinder – the cube dug out to form a canopy, the cylinder left solid to make the entrance hall. Here, too, was the manifestation of a traditional theme which the Villa Savoye had revealed. The Villa was like a prototype for larger schemes; it provided Le Corbusier with a situation where he could work out architectural principles. Palladio's Villa Capra could also be regarded as a prototype, insofar as others perceived its message and gave the architectural principles he set down there a wider range. The principles conveyed by the Salvation Army building, like the Villa Savoye, are similar to those conveyed by the Piazza Navona – there is the vitality of life in the cube and the cylinder in the foreground, there is the great calm glass façade, plainer than anything comparable devised by Mies van der Rohe, and there is the outbreak of jagged shapes of the roof-top. The combination of all these things – the neutrality and the acrobatics – explains the idea of the building, and hammers home a theme that is central to architecture.

The Salvation Army hostel is part of a city, and part of something infinitely larger than itself. Clearly an individual structure of this kind must accept the life of this city, and adjust to it, and the complexities in the foreground are symbolic of this life, in the same way that the glass façade, through its neutrality, takes note of, and respects, the presence of its neighbours. In a sense, the building is unfinished and must be finished by others, in this case by the architectural objects in the foreground. The glass back-drop is the frame, and this and its variations had become the theme of Le Corbusier's architecture: a frame and its subsequent variations are a theme of architecture – ancient Greece, Roman, eighteenth-century English, the eastern roof and courtyard. Architecture is like a stage with its proscenium and scenery, and within this proscenium and in front of this scenery, people act out their lives. By the mid-1930s Le Corbusier had mastered this theme, he understood its consequences and knew what it meant in terms of town planning. But while, on one level, these revelations were taking place, the research, on another, was continuing relentlessly: the 'storehouse of inspiration' was filling up.

He had built in concrete, changed to steel, used glass, discovered glass bricks and invented *brise soleil* (louvred shutters to diffuse glare) for the Rio building. Now stone started to appear, *piloti* (columns) disappeared, walls were rooted to the ground, grass grew on vaulted roofs. And there were some words he wrote in a letter to some students: 'I wish that sometimes architects would take up their pencils to draw a plant or a leaf, or to express the significance of the clouds, the ever-changing ebb and flow of waves at play upon the sands. . . .'

His paintings had changed, too, they were softer, rounder, the edges to the shapes were blurred, there were shadows among the light (*see Plate 15*). Something was about to happen. And then, in the middle 1940s, it happened. Le Corbusier invented the Modulor, a form of measure that introduced a new range of proportions that were, like the Greek diagram (but much more elaborate) derived from the proportions of the human figure (*see Plate 13*). This invention was momentous because it heralded the beginning of a new phase in his work. His increasing preoccupation with nature, which ran parallel to a decreasing interest in the industrialized aesthetic, required a focus, and this focus had to be man, the human figure, its shape and proportions – in other words, the Modulor. This measure was again a frame, for it gave order, and offered him the greater freedom he had discovered in painting, perceived in nature and longed to bring to his architecture.

As much as any building, any painting or drawing, the Modulor seems to convey a vivid picture of its creator: the Modulor is like an imprint of the man. What *was* he like? As he appeared to the world, austere, with a big head and big features, in some way not dissimilar to Derain, a look of disdain partly hidden behind the thick glasses with their heavy, black frames. He was a great patriot, but the subject of his patriotism was art, not a country. At first glance, he seemed to be possibly a scientist, certainly a highbrow; without question dynamic, a man with relentless energy and drive; hypersensitive, perhaps, an innocent, and with a faith and sense of purpose not unlike Eliot's; but essentially a man of his times – the 1920s. Yet there was also the private person who was, somehow, despite a certain peasant roughness, intensely touching and warm and human – the man whom friends called Corbu, and who was described by them as exquisitely kind, generous and unselfish: and one thinks of the *chaise-longue* at the end of the bath at the Villa Savoye, and his excitement when he embraced a column at La Tourette, and the gentle way he held his pencils, and his coloured glass suns shining orange into his chapel at Ronchamp, and the photograph of him under his hat in the hot sun at Chandigarh, and Madame Corbusier shouting through the pivotted door of his studio overlooking the Bois, 'Mr Modulor, your lunch is getting cold.'

3   Last Themes

It is to Le Corbusier's small buildings that one invariably turns for the clues that will break the code of his larger designs and huge conceptions: then one may get the message and discover the treasure. Similarly, it is to the smaller buildings that one looks for a pointer that will suggest what might have been turning over in his mind at a particular time, in the same way that one looks at his paintings and drawings to see if they convey the spirit of what he was building, or was about to build: for Le Corbusier painted every morning in his studio in his flat overlooking the Bois, and worked on his buildings for the rest of the day in his office at Rue de Sèvres. Painting is thus an important guide: for Le Corbusier, painting and architecture were one. His writing is, however, another guide to his thoughts – his books, of course, but also the occasional letter, the odd conversation, remark or word. Anything he said or did may have great bearing on his buildings.

The small designs are like the short comment or letter; and they are, too, like seeds scattered about from which some huge and wonderful plant will some day grow. Le Corbusier's last large works of the thirties were completed around 1934 – this was the year the flats in Paris were finished. He discovered glass bricks in Belgium at a house built in 1910 by the Art Nouveau architect Antoine Pompe, and, after some correspondence with this man, used them at the *Pavillon Suisse*. Then, rather like Picasso who went through a phase when he used the colour green over and over again until he had got it out of his system, he saturated with glass bricks four of the five large buildings that were squeezed into the three years following the building of the Villa Savoye. They cover the ground floor of the Salvation

Army hostel, they light the staircase at the *Pavillon Suisse*, they construct the landings and flights of steps at the Geneva flats (to bring light from the top of the building to the bottom), and they make the balconies of the flats in Paris, where he himself lived in a penthouse. Who would have thought of making a glass brick staircase, or a glass brick façade? Le Corbusier did and, in consequence, glass bricks became the latest modern architectural fashion of the day. He also discovered stone at the *Pavillon Suisse*, but used it in a random, rural way that made a sharp note of contrast with the smooth stone and glass facing on the main building. And rough stone also crept into his studio in the flats on the Bois; and the ceiling was curved – another departure from earlier buildings.

But then there was a curious gap of about twelve years in which he built nothing of any size at all. He went on painting and writing, designed and laid out another volume in his series of books, and preoccupied himself with town planning projects. A competition scheme for an office block in Zurich was rejected because it was 'too modern', and his other work was centred on ideas for housing in Algiers and a glass skyscraper that would suit any large and congested city. In all these schemes Le Corbusier was developing possibilities that had arisen from the *Pavillon Suisse*, some of the early houses and other buildings – playing with glass, steel, concrete, and variations with volumes but always within the precise limits of a predetermined aesthetic frame. There was, however, a parallel development under way. While these elaborate schemes for housing and the skyscraper were being publicized and around the time the glass of the *Pavillon Suisse* must have been going into place, a villa for a woman named Madame de Mondrot was built near Toulon. This was in 1931. The design showed a total break with everything else he was doing at that time. The house had a rambling plan, it was made with rough stone that was whitewashed in places, and the windows were wood; with its straight flight of steps into the garden it captured the atmosphere of a local style. And this led on to something else : three years later a tiny cottage that was called a week-end house appeared. This was a beautiful little building. It was as though Le Corbusier had put away his vast endeavours for a couple of moments to study the source, the minutiae of which town plans are composed, the realities and not the dangerous abstractions of the problem – in other words, the business of living in a very small space.

Le Corbusier says at one point that 'architecture and town planning go hand-in-hand'. They do; the true meaning of town planning – nowadays blurred by the innumerable allied departments of planning (sociological, economic, geographical and the rest) – is the use of buildings, and the arrangement of spaces between buildings, to make ordered and imaginative surroundings or environments. And so town planning is based on the architectural quality of buildings of one kind and another, and on the arrangement of these buildings, with the major element of this composition being residential. It is the architect, therefore, who makes the environment, and so, to understand town planning and all its ramifications, he has to go back to the house, or at least to surroundings for living. Although Le Corbusier's mind was engaged on bigger things than individual houses like the Villas Cook, Stein and Savoye – themselves useful research for what came after them – he must have seized on the week-end house with relish. For it was real research, and not a project; it brought him sharply back to the beginning again, as the Modulor was to do later. But the week-end house, like the Mondrot Villa, was completely different from anything he had done before : no *piloti*, no flat top, no influence of the industrialized aesthetic. It was as though Le Corbusier had collected some notes, thoughts and favourite materials – glass bricks from his flats, the curved ceiling and rough stone from his studio – and had put them down at the week-end house. This time the research was into natural materials, a closer relation-

ship with nature, and forms that arose from this relationship: hence the vaulted roof and the grass growing out of
it, the plywood ceilings bent to follow the shape of the
vaults, and the rough stone walls.

Although the hold of the cube, as it was employed at the
Villa Savoye, has been considerably loosened, the spirit of
this form still survives: it can, for instance, be perceived in
the plan, which is roughly square, but with parts of the
square removed to let the light and the garden into the
centre of the house. This recalls the theme on the back of
the watch where parts of the formal pattern were left out
to encourage the presence of nature. Le Corbusier opens the
door to nature in the same sort of way at the week-end
house: three bits of the square have disappeared, and the
plan, like a piece of geometric jigsaw, snaps neatly into a
position which exactly fits the natural random forms of the
scene around. Contrast partly explains the perfection of the
fit: this irregular object is as precise and sharp as an ice-
cube. Le Corbusier had brought the delicacy and refinement
of his architecture to nature – there was none of the earthy
rustic roughness that characterizes the nature-loving early
houses of Frank Lloyd Wright, who deliberately sought to
smudge the boundary between the building and the landscape. This hint of sentimentality about natural things was
totally alien to Le Corbusier, not a suggestion of it touched
any part of his forms, nothing was allowed to reduce the
stature of architecture; respect for buildings meant respect
for people, and, with Le Corbusier, people came before
nature.

The weekend house announced a new phase: for although a condition of the design was that it should be very
private (and Le Corbusier duly hid the building), everything
about this house connects with a growing feeling for nature
– its shape, softness, a closeness to the earth. The structure
was hidden behind a bank, and the concrete vaults open out
of the bank – white and clear and strong – like entrances to
a cave in a chalk cliff. The cube and its various ramifica-

tions were no longer required to act as an aesthetic frame, or discipline; the roof vault had replaced the cube – repeated, it is the vault which acts as the frame for the whole composition. Shaped as an arch, and, in sympathy with the banks and mounds round about, the vault naturally accepts the irregular form of the plan because these irregularities follow the direction of the vaults. Le Corbusier was only taking a lesson from traditional tiled roofs here: the Roman tiles, for instance, are semi-circular in shape and perhaps six inches across, but when they are repeated in their thousands over a roof they produce a succession of hundreds of parallel lines running from the ridge down to the eaves. The strong sunshine of the southern climates where they are used in Europe brings out their shape and stresses, through shadows, the lines. Because the lines are so strongly emphasized all kinds of irregularities along the length of the eaves are possible – they pass unnoticed, or they seem very pleasant, fitting in with the irregularities of the countryside. But in architectural terms the lines are acting as a frame which accepts the irregularities which follow, like Le Corbusier's vaults, the direction of the tiles, of which they are merely a visual projection.

Le Corbusier would have immediately seen the possibilities of the tiles used in another way, just as he saw immense possibilities in their enlargement as vaults; and, by seeing the possibilities of the vault, and by using it in a new way, he draws attention to the meaning and importance of the tile in traditional architecture. And he was so delighted with his discovery that, rather as all structures became arches when the Romans discovered the arch, all roofs became vaults when he found the barrel vault. Vaults were, from this moment on in 1935, an insistent theme in his work, as the cube, concrete, glass and horizontal windows had been before them. This, of course, doesn't mean that he had discarded the precious discoveries of the past – they were still on hand, in and out of the 'storehouse' as circumstances demanded, ready for use when the right opportunity suggested itself. Le Corbusier merely had a wider range and variety of forms, parts and materials to choose from; and the greater the range, the greater the room for manoeuvre, the more flexible, the more free became his approach to buildings. At the weekend house it is, in fact, the combination of the vault and the cube that conjures up such a perfect balance between order and freedom, with the vault in full control and the cube taking up a somewhat secondary position – its presence is inferred, no longer stated. But there is, nevertheless, a reminder of the past at the bottom of the path in a separate, square structure with a single vault supported on four columns; the clue that Le Corbusier left behind – a memorial perhaps to his early inspiration and former, beloved master.

Cézanne said he 'perceived Nature rather late'. This could be said of Le Corbusier as well – possibly the classical tradition held them both back. For when, in his letter to the students, Le Corbusier talked about 'undertaking voyages of discovery into the inexhaustible domain of nature' he was in his late forties, or about the same age as Cézanne. If, for Le Corbusier, an understanding of nature meant freedom based on the structure, order and economy that he had first observed in the fir trees of the Jura mountains when he was a boy, and on the limitless variations within this structure, order and economy, why shouldn't the spirit of this freedom be transferred to architecture? The phenomena of architecture – the frame, the forms that have endured over thousands of precarious years, the capitals of the five ancient orders – evolved from associations with nature in the first place, from the earliest structures of reeds and rushes and sticks, the forms of which were themselves adaptations of nature. Why should these origins not continue to be a source of inspiration, and the spirit of their traditions not continue to assist in the present as those of ancient Greece had done? In other words, Le Corbusier was no longer content to study just the Greek mind, but was now interested in the mind which preceded it; he was interested, so to speak, in the pre-birth situation as a source of imagery. At the weekend house, for instance, he seems to have been inspired by the cave. Well, why not? The cave had made a wonderful natural home, and it inspired the Middle Eastern hunter of ten or eleven thousand years ago when he transformed the mouth of the cave – the semi-circular outline – into a three-dimensional form – the bee-hive hut – and this was indeed a brainwave. The weekend house suggests a cave, too; it is a hollow with light at one end. The sides of the house – stone, glass bricks – emphasize this source of light, and the view of green leaves and grass at the end of the vaults is like a picture seen from inside a cave. But then, again, the inspiration for this house cannot be separated from other associations – the burrow, even the anthill – which the imagery also suggests.

Le Corbusier had this extraordinary gift for soaking up everything around him, and for seeing how ideas used in one situation could be changed for use in another, in this way gaining a spectacular identity. Some drawings by him of the reconstruction of a primitive temple in *Towards a New Architecture*, and thoughts he must have been turning over in his mind about this temple, could, for example, have led to the structure of a tent he designed for the Paris exhibition ten years later in the middle 1930s which was regarded as a feat of modern technology. The structural principles were similar: canvas roofs prevented from sagging by restraining cords (in his case, wires) that were in tension. But the weekend house had more tangible origins. The materials were traditional – stone, wood, brick, tiles: they belonged to the trees and the earth outside and represented a total reversal of all he worked with before. His inspiration seemed to lie, more and more, with natural things. A snail inspired the idea for a museum he designed at this time, a stone found on the beach at Cap Martin inspired a long series of paintings, the fir tree (and the curious resemblance between the structure of a leaf and the structure of the tree to which the leaf belonged) partly inspired the Modulor. Similarly, the rough farm buildings of southern France inspired the stone and wood holiday house at Mathés, where a corrugated iron roof changed places with traditional tiles, thus suggesting, with corrugation, the character of a tile with another material. Yet – and this is the point that has to be stressed – the house lost none of the impetus of Le Corbusier's modern architectural imagery because of a growing interest in traditional materials; he was saying the same things in a different way – and this, in harmony with rural traditions, sharpened up the contrasts of large, heavy walls and open interiors with their big windows.

Le Corbusier said : 'If you have a pencil in your hand ... you will understand many things; you now have a stock of eloquent values which are the lesson of natural phenomena.' He was referring to objects which, like pebbles, are scattered everywhere. The local Moorish architecture of north Africa, for instance, fascinated him; he had made dozens of notes about it, and out of these the vault again emerged. In the early 1940s he designed an elaborate house on the coast there which was to be built by primitive means and native labour. Le Corbusier's comments are as significant as ever : 'The building is in accordance with landscape, climate and tradition !' For the undulations of the vaults echoed the profiles of the hills and islands in the sea; the structure – high and open – was conceived as a shelter from the sun and wind; and the materials and character were in accord with the indigenous style of the country. He seemed to be celebrating his freedom from classical disciplines; the ideas that were set out in the little weekend house – the ease of movement induced by the vault – were put to work on a much bigger scale; and the combination of the irregularities of the building and the high boundary wall created a casual but ordered arrangement of rooms round courtyards – so casual that the house has the air of having been added to, of having grown in size over a number of years, in the way that old houses do naturally grow, with a wing here, an extension there, and pleasant garden court-yards with trees happening between them. Le Corbusier thus captured in this house the spirit of slowly evolving forms, and he did this by describing, with accuracy and great attention to detail, special characteristics he had no-ticed in the buildings of the locality. Yet the architectural elements which hold the composition together are as strongly stated as ever. Two aesthetic frames were at work; there are the vaults, sliding backwards and forwards ac-cording to the will of the spaces below them, that frame the volumes in one direction, and there is the perimeter wall (all that is left of the sides of the square form that ordered the Villa Savoye) that contains the volumes in the other direction. Thus there are two images, the one superimposed on the other. In one, there are rooms round courts, garden walls and palm trees (a relaxed domestic scene of a rural kind); in the other, the whole conception – with its solids and voids, and roofs rippling along tops of walls – is a piece of sculpture made of mud bricks and a coat of whitewash, and exquisitely rough and fresh.

These two images combine to suggest where Le Cor-busier was going – that the barriers created by classical disciplines were dissolving, that he felt it was necessary to go further back in search of wisdom, to essentials, if he was to go forward again. As an artist Le Corbusier needed more material to draw on : the classical heritage, in the being of the Acropolis, had started him off with his first themes, but this was no longer enough to sustain the momentum of what he had to do. It is a human instinct to simplify and Le Corbusier's work demonstrates a steady process of simpli-fication. The Parthenon, in a sense, was the conclusion of others, and, if he was to get to the heart of the matter, Le Corbusier had to get back to man, to the human being in its primitive state, stripped of possessions. This meant getting down to the bare essentials of building and putting aside, for the time being, the knowledge of the twentieth century. Six years of war had stripped him of his possessions (his flat in Paris, his office in Rue de Sèvres) and gave him time to think. He was going through a period of renewal. His ceaselessly creative 'storehouse for inspiration' was stocking up. What are the bare essentials of architecture but those provided by the aesthetic frame? What is a structure but a floor to lift you up and a roof to cover you?

But the dimensions of an aesthetic frame are determined by the dimensions of man and the space he occupies. Without these dimensions, Le Corbusier would have said, there is architectural anarchy. And so, in the 1940s, at the time when his discovery of the barrel vault had really gripped him, he invented a measure that would establish these dimensions: the Modulor, the crystallization of an idea that had accompanied him throughout his life (*see Plate 13*). The basis and functions of this he explains in his books. The design of these, the layout of photographs and drawings, were Le Corbusier's own and these publications are thus of particular importance. For instance, in *My Work* on the same page as the pocket watch, there appears a series of drawings of fir trees. In some of these drawings the branches are covered in the snow of the 'rugged winters' of La Chaux-de-Fonds, but one consists of a diagram of the tree's structure. Then you notice that the design of the watch and the picture of the tree, made at about the same time, are really part of each other; the formal pattern of the watch is like the tree's trunk and branches – both provide a structure which carries the foliage. 'That intractable tree,' comments Le Corbusier, and then goes on to say that, in a purely accidental and spontaneous way, it guided him 'as far back as 1904 to considerations of a mathematical kind which were to lead forty years later to the Modulor'.

In retrospect the Modulor was a logical and key step in Le Corbusier's development: he invented it when he needed it, as the Greeks had invented their diagram of proportion when this was needed. Like all tools, it was a product of circumstances and, as such, could not have been invented at any other time. Before, he had relied on his studies of classical disciplines for guidance; now that he was seeking a greater freedom that he had perceived in nature, it was to the conception of man in space that he turned. For man was the measure that possessed the discipline that provided the freedom: thus man and nature merge – like the two halves of the circular symbol of the mandala, they balance each other, they are inseparable: nature's underlying order and man's simplified order are both distilled there, in the invention, as part of each other, as they are in life. 'Man must be rediscovered', Le Corbusier writes. And elsewhere: 'I admired the house of peasants, the house of men, the shack, the thing that is modest and on a human scale. That is where I invented a part of the Modulor, discovering human dimensions in things of total simplicity. . . .' Yet the invention of the Modulor, like the rediscovery of the frame, leapt across two thousand years to establish a physical link with ancient Greece.

The Modulor was, of course, a different conception to the Greek diagram of proportion, and this was precisely because Le Corbusier came to it from his own personal research and experience. The circle had no part in the Modulor: its measures were determined by height which character- ized the space occupied by a man six foot tall. Yet the navel is again the centre-line of the diagram, giving a measure of 113 centimetres from the ground; and the top of the upstretched arm gives the total vertical measurement of 226 centimetres – and thus, inevitably, the double cube. But a number of other variations gave Le Corbusier's system a far greater range than the Greek method, and thus far greater flexibility to meet the innumerable variations of modern situations. Other horizontals were introduced by the top of a man's head, by the seat of a chair in a relaxed position (and again for the upright and conventional posi- tion – eating, for instance), by the average height of the elbow when working, and so on. The diagram could then be divided vertically on the centre-line of the figure, creating further proportions, and these could then be sub-divided. Le

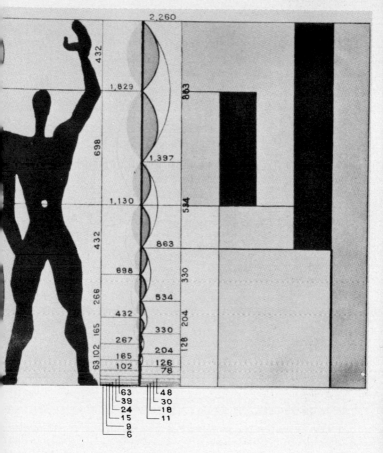

13 The Modulor: Le Corbusier's diagram of human proportion
published in 1946

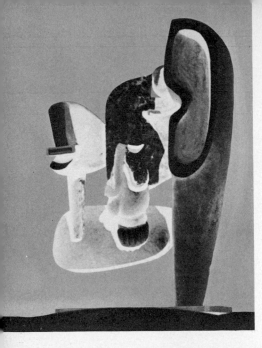

14 Sculpture of the ear i
polychrome, 1945. Le
Corbusier particularly
liked this picture
15 A painting of the lat
1930s

16 *Opposite:* *L'Unité
d'habitation* at
Marseilles

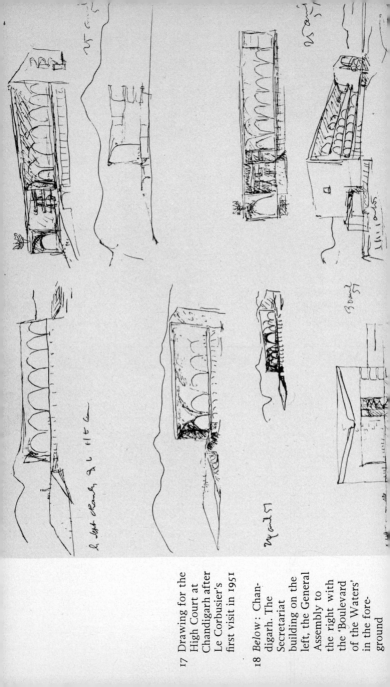

17 Drawing for the High Court at Chandigarh after Le Corbusier's first visit in 1951

18 *Below:* Chandigarh. The Secretariat building on the left, the General Assembly to the right with the 'Boulevard of the Waters' in the foreground

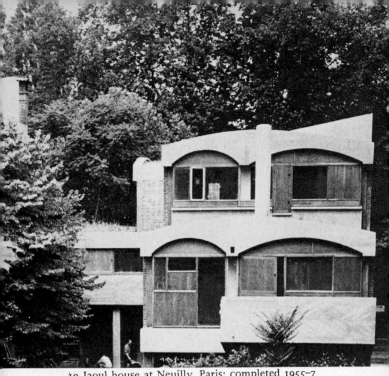

19 Jaoul house at Neuilly, Paris; completed 1955-7

20 The 'mandala' diagram of day and night, 1950

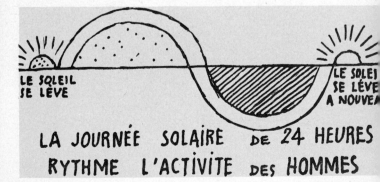

LE SOLEIL SE LÈVE

LE SOLEIL SE LÈVE A NOUVEAU

LA JOURNÉE SOLAIRE DE 24 HEURES RYTHME L'ACTIVITÉ DES HOMMES

21 The Corbusier
Centre at
Zürich, com-
pleted in 1968

22 Monastery of Sainte-
Marie de la Tourette
at Eveux, Lyons;
completed in 1960

23 Picasso standing figu

Corbusier's system was thus similar to the classical method insofar as it relied on the dimensions of the human figure; but it also represented the human being in movement within the space it occupies. This was the Modulor. The invention was announced in 1947 and described in a book published a year later. Le Corbusier called it an essential guide in an age of prefabrication and industrialized techniques of building. He recognized the dangers of the machine, and called in the Modulor – which tied buildings back to the scale of the human being – as a practical way of actively resisting its threat. In a sense, then, this invention echoed fears that are now becoming universal. From Le Corbusier's point of view, however, he had made another discovery. In the centre was man, represented by the Modulor, holding the huge, diverse and complex structure together: Le Corbusier's preoccupation with nature, with painting, with indigenous building techniques, and with a much greater freedom of form.

Briefly, this invention meant that Le Corbusier was able to continue his pursuit of more ambitious objectives; and now, too, more by suggestion than by persuasion, the search for an aesthetic order could go on, and be accomplished, the more insistent classical disciplines having been shed. This theme, first sensed in the fir tree, had by now been gathering momentum for some time. There is evidence of it in the 1920s when he designed the Vertical Garden City which, he said, creates 'a real landscape and provides the opportunity of admiring it, by means of eloquent avenues superimposed one upon the other'. He could see his garden city absolutely clearly; much changed, it eventually led to the *L'Unité d'habitation* at Marseilles. But the fir tree was also an important factor in the history of this building. In the first place, it helped to inspire the Modulor. It was, however, a significant addition to his collection of things that included shells, pebbles, bits of wood, fossils, stone chips and a meat-bone. And in one of his later books he makes a visual observation that may have been suggested by the fir – a series of drawings appear on consecutive pages which show that the leaf has a structure and shape identical to the tree to which it presumably belongs. The leaf thus has an intimate relationship with the tree; and, repeated thousands of times, it gives the tree its form. This process of construction could be compared to the architectural and physical construction of the *L'Unité d'habitation*, the proportion of which was directed by the Modulor (*see Plate 16*). The leaf can be exchanged for the human being who is surrounded by a space (his home), the proportion of which is derived from his size. The repetition of homes construct the *L'Unité* which, as the tree is to the leaf, is directly related by proportion to the home, and to the human being. Thus we begin to see what he means when he says that the fir tree, in particular, inspired the Modulor. 'One thing suggests another,' Le Corbusier said simply. A further analogy with the tree again emerges from more drawings of the same period. This time the branches with their maze of twigs feeding the leaves with nourishment are compared to the maze of veins in the heart: the heart needs oxygen as the tree needs fresh air and sunshine. Similarly the *L'Unité* needs fresh air and sunshine, and thus its façades have an aerated appearance, opening up to the skies with the deep breaths of private terraces, one to each apartment.

But then Le Corbusier goes on to explain the principles governing the conception of the *L'Unité* in another way, as they are related to man. As he said earlier, there is no such thing as primitive man – merely primitive resources. So he takes a native hut, a nomadic tent, a bottle and an individual apartment from the *L'Unité*. He claims that the hut, the tent, the bottle and the apartment are connected, and that they lead logically to the *L'Unité*. All are shown on their own, isolated from their neighbours, the apartment as well – he has drawn some trees round it to make this quite clear. On the one hand he seems to be saying that all four represent the bare essentials of life – a roof to cover you, a space to live, somewhere to eat and drink. On another level, however, he seems to be saying that, while all four diagrams represent enclosures of some kind or another, the hut and the tent lack a community frame as the bottle lacks a stand into which it and other bottles can be stacked together. He is thus comparing the structure of the *L'Unité* to a bottle-stand into which he can slide the apartments, bringing the hut and the tent (the bare essentials of life) together under the shelter of one roof, and uniting families within one frame: hence, *L'Unité*. What he is saying, then, is that the hut is an apartment (and that, in its time, it was a good one), but that it should have an ordered relationship with the next hut; and that, if it is one among innumerable huts, like houses in a town, its form must be simplified because it is part of something which is far larger than itself; that it is part of a community, and it must, therefore, adjust itself to the aesthetic laws that govern the community as a whole. In architecture these laws show themselves in an ordered relationship of parts within an overall aesthetic frame. Without this order there is anarchy. A village should have this order, so should a town, and a district within the town. The *L'Unité* is like a town. It has its shops, its streets, its nursery school and a public garden on the roof: the town is contained within the framework of one building, like bottles in a stand. Le Corbusier called his *L'Unité* the 'green town'.

And so, in these lovely little pen drawings, there is a diagram of the evolution of the town from nomadic days. We are back with the frame again – the frame that ordered the mandala pattern of the watch, that decided the shape of the *Ateliers d'Artistes*, that reduced the intricate interlocking works of the Villa Savoye to a single object. But now the frame has been given a far greater range, for it has taken over the town and given shape to the community.

In a large composition like a town, however, the frame relates to the whole rather than to the parts (the houses) and, for this reason, becomes a more distant presence, although still fully in control; a comprehensible diagram within which there are the variations. In other words buildings and open space are to this larger frame what doors and windows are to the frame of a single building. The instinct for simplification created the ancient Greek frame; on a much larger scale, it creates the *L'Unité*'s frame, in the same way that it created the urban frame for eighteenth-century English architecture. As in painting, the greater the composition's scale, the simpler must be the detail, tone and colour : in a large building, the scale of every part of the composition is raised to a point where each has a natural and decisive relationship to the whole – this is what Andrea Palladio meant when he wrote about the relationship of parts. Ultimately, however, the scale of architecture can only be related to one thing – the dimensions and proportion of the human being. The scale and the proportion of the *L'Unité* is thus directed by the Modulor, from the length and height of the building down to the smallest details of balconies and cupboards. It is this invention which made Le Corbusier's *L'Unité* possible, and the relationship of every part mathematically exact; and it is this mathematical exactness which holds the entire picture as closely together, and as firmly, as a perfectly constructed piece of furniture. Only a measure that was far in advance of the Greek diagram of proportion could have regulated the design of such a highly complex problem, and could have simplified its solution so completely.

The variations creep back through the terraces that extend the full two storeys of the living space thus abruptly shrinking the apparent size of the block from the outside; through the bedroom windows that are narrow slits; through the band of shops on the ninth and tenth floors; through the *piloti* at the base, and the eruptions of sculptural forms on the top – the tall lift and water towers, the sloping roof of the gymnasium, and the cantilevered projections from which the entire face of the *L'Unité* can be seen from above. But variations also creep in through the casting of

the concrete. When Le Corbusier was commissioned to design the building the war had, of course, just ended. Money,
steel and skilled craftsmen were in short supply. At the
same time the climate is a hot one and the landscape is
bare. Such limitations and conditions suggested a new kind
of concrete imagery, and he called this *béton brut*, and
brut, translated, means raw. Thus *béton brut* (which had
nothing to do with the fashionable journalese of English
'New Brutalism' of the 1950s) described the exact impression left on concrete by wooden shuttering – the lines of the
planks and their grain – and this impression was, as such,
a precise representation of natural materials. This rough
patterning introduced a texture to the building that had a
primitive, natural and warm quality which suited local
Mediterranean building methods and, when combined with
the bright colours Le Corbusier used on balconies, the glare
of the sun in the raw landscape. Brought to the more subtle
light and the highly industrialized countries of the north,
béton brut made no sense at all, but Le Corbusier's change
of style had a lightning effect on his followers nevertheless :
it was copied everywhere and brute concrete became the
order of the day. The *L'Unité* had, in fact, a far greater
influence than predecessors like the Villas Stein and Savoye
of the early days, and the consequences of its influence
were, on the whole, disastrous : in copying the appearances
of his work, the imitators failed to recognize the underlying
principles that governed it, and, in a way that has happened
over and over again in the history of architecture, they
turned those appearances into a style which, in its last stages
of debasement, become a uniform of the dullest kind :
it has nothing to do with Le Corbusier at all. But the imitators were wrong on another count as well. The *L'Unité* does
not present a change of style. On the contrary, Le Corbusier
had merely picked up a theme at a point where he had had
to leave off before the war – with the weekend house, the
holiday house at Mathés, the vaults and the rough stone-

work – and, at the *L'Unité*, he was continuing to develop this theme with his usual determination.

The vaults reappear in a project for some houses on a hillside at Cap Martin, but this was never built. They appear again at the Jaoul house in Neuilly (*see Plate 19*), finished in 1956, and these give away the reason, if anything does, why Le Corbusier shed the austerity of the classical discipline in the end: surely there was a deeply emotional man trying to get out of the strait-jacket? The voluptuous shapes and sensual struggle at Jaoul, suggested by Le Corbusier's later painting, but never fully communicated by them, and imagined out of such a seemingly casual and simple plan, have great power. Rough with rugged concrete and brick, jagged with windows, this building assaults the spectator; but the violence you experience gives real pleasure – the irresistible pleasure of curves, surface sensations and rhythmic movements, of provocative and sexy water spouts – that was seldom allowed a public performance.

Le Corbusier preferred to serve the public rather than himself. Yet here, at Jaoul, some closely guarded secret got away. For all that, and transcending it, the same search for a human simplicity in natural forms and materials was going on relentlessly. The shape of the glorious vaults recalls the microscopic biological studies he made of veins in the human heart – and which themselves resemble the snow-laden boughs of the fir tree drawn when he was a boy – in working out ideas for the *L'Unité d'habitation*; and the monastic, white interiors with splashes of grass green embody the spirit of the primitive native hut and peasant's house which helped to lead him to the Modulor. 'Peasant art is a striking creation of aesthetic sensuality,' Le Corbusier said. Here, at the Jaoul house, he had taken another risk; and here, too, was something of the distinctive taste that was to come later at Chandigarh, in India.

The greatest risk Le Corbusier ever took was in the Chapel of Notre Dame du Haut at Ronchamp. This extraordinary building was finished after the *L'Unité* at Marseilles and two years before the Jaoul house. But startling and original though the chapel is, this building cannot be separated from everything else he did, whether of the past or future, the Villa Stein, the monastery of La Tourette, or the research of the post-war years, any more than it can be separated from his memories of the Greek islands and his paintings.

In Le Corbusier's own words the Chapel was 'totally free architecture. . . .' It was a design that was entirely in harmony with nature. The atmosphere that surrounds it is thick with associations: they flicker through the mind like hosts of flashbacks, so fast they are almost subliminal – a storehouse in the Ardèche, a marrow bone, Le Thoronet smiling over the top of a wooded hill and the severe stone and round towers of its sister abbey of Sénanque, music and his mother, sounds and cylinders, Bellevue, the shape of guns, the water spouts at Venasque and at the Palais des Papes at Avignon, a crab's shell, a drawing made from a passing train of the ruined chapel that had been bombed in the war – only the tower was still standing. These associations and others – the underground cathedral at St. Emilion and Le Corbusier's underground design for a basilica at Sainte-Baume – impose almost a visible pattern at Ronchamp. Le Corbusier captured the moment of genius in which the building was conceived and he never released that moment (*see Plate 5*). Only three weeks after visiting Ronchamp on May 20th in 1950 he had put down a clear impression of the chapel that was finally built. It was all there, in that rather smudgy drawing, as he said, at 'one stroke' – the towers, the enormous roof the sweeping wall freckled with odd shaped windows; as though he had recorded, in the flash for one occasion, a lifetime of sensations and associations, experiences and ideas. Perhaps this is why the building conveys such a profusion of images. But when the atmosphere surrounding this pure building of the imagination evaporates it leaves behind a single, white crystal: Ronchamp.

The Chapel recalls Sainte-Baume, designed two years be
fore, because it crowns the top of a hill, over which i
smiles like Le Thoronet, somehow suggesting an under
ground cavern below that might be the continuation of ai
idea inspired by the cathedral at St Emilion. Yet it recalls
too, the geometric exactness of Sénanque, and the loftines
of this abbey's cool, sheer, creamy walls. At Sénanque th
architecture is boiled down to the stone bones and strippe(
of all decorative possessions – nothing is extraneous tc
form; the deep windows, like those at Ronchamp, are s(
precisely made that they might have been taken out of th
solid by a very sharp chisel. But the image of Ronchamp ii
these windows is superceded by another – the deep win
dows of ordinary peasant architecture in villages and farm
houses, blurred and rough with painted outlines, which th
windows of Sénanque and Ronchamp pull into precise ai
chitectural focus. And so you see that, between the abbe
and the indigenous style of the region, Le Corbusier's im
ages overlap in all directions. A single column that you fin(
in a vaulted structure, around which there is a free arrang(
ment of spaces, could be compared to the single colum;
in the kitchen at La Tourette, the presence of which was s
powerful that Le Corbusier embraced it at first sight; yet th
cylindrical forms at Sénanque also recall the clover leaf pla
of the Romanesque baptistry at Venasque, and the stor
towers of châteaux, and of the country house. Thus the cy
indrical light shafts at Ronchamp are, like some wine,
theme of the country – as, of course, Cézanne's *Pigeo*
Tower at Bellevue turns out to be; and you discover tha
these light shafts do, after all, have the same origins as th
main body of the building, belonging to the same jigsav
Southern French architecture *is* curvaceous, and this chara(
teristic is often reflected in the vertical plane of houses whet
plastered coatings spread outwards as they near the groun(
following the batters at the base of fortresses and château:
There is a memory of this tradition at Ronchamp, too : th
plan of the flowing south wall is shaped in the section, s

that this form, with its hints of the snow-laden boughs of the firs, also spreads at the base. Le Corbusier captures the locality in this single gesture. It is for this reason, among others, that the Chapel belongs so totally to the locality, in the same way that simultaneously (and, it seems, almost by chance) the light shafts pick up a nun's shape in whitewash.

But at this point Le Corbusier's paintings and sculptures should be studied: in these, he was investigating a theme which has, in the context of Ronchamp, a rather special significance. In 1948, or thereabouts, he began working on a series of sculptures in polychrome. The theme was ears, and this suggests the sounds and acoustics which so absorbed him. His interest in the ear shows from far back in 1929 when he drew *Josephine*. But the idea for the sculpture came from some paintings and drawings Le Corbusier had been doing in the early 1940s. This is interesting because it shows how close to sculpture both his paintings and buildings were – Ronchamp was partly suggested by the sculpture, and by his paintings. But so far as Le Corbusier was concerned there was no clear dividing line between painting, drawing, sculpture and buildings, and the model of Ronchamp made in 1950 was also a piece of sculpture. They were simply different parts of one activity. In 1944 Le Corbusier did a drawing of a head with a huge ear that resembled the handle of a cup – and, more particularly, a cup (or glass) drawn by him in the early 1920s. A friend named Joseph Savina, who was just back from a prison camp in Germany, suggested that sculpture should be made from his drawings and paintings of the ears. Le Corbusier was amazed but, predictably, fell in with the plan. Savina was a good sculptor himself and a superb craftsman with wood. And so these very strange, tall, listening ears began to appear.

The ear, in the first pieces, was on the top of a long neck. There was a tension in the muscles of that neck which stressed the concentration exerted by the act of listening, as though for distant sounds of the sea in a shell, or for a bird

rustling in the undergrowth; and the ear, in the shape of a
question mark, expressed a peculiarly apprehensive air, like
the roving, sensitive listening apparatus of a radar receiver
revolving on a hill somewhere. Sometimes the ears, made in
polychrome (a form of clay), were unpainted; sometimes,
however, they were brightly coloured, and this transformed
them into curious creatures with interests other than listening – into something like birds, even crow-like perhaps. And
sometimes the ears were put with other forms (*see Plate
14*), the combination of which suggested a complete head, a
second ear also listening, but shaped differently, like a
marrow-bone. The first of these sculptures were, nevertheless, generally concerned with the solitary object, the ear on
a tall neck, although in some cases two ears listened in
opposite directions on the same stand, or were contained
inside a square frame. And these were the pieces he was
working on, and Savina was making in Brittany, when the
Chapel at Ronchamp was conceived in 1950.

Le Corbusier was also painting. By now, of course, all the
machine symbolism had vanished from his pictures, his
shapes were free and flowing, and, without exception
centred in some way on figures – on the human being. This
was in complete contrast to the paintings he had done
twenty years earlier, which were focussed on the machine:
one called *With Many Objects*, done in 1925, with the
merest suggestion of an architectural form in the back
ground to act as a frame, might have been prompted by the
kind of way he saw the Villa Savoye – as a tight relation
ship of parts interlocking like wheels in a watch and en
closed by the simple classical square. But there was no
formal regularity in the paintings and drawings of the 1940
– then, shapes and colours were floating among long and per
fect lines: all that is left of the early days is the perfection
of the line. And the line, the absolute precision of it, was of
total importance to Le Corbusier, both in painting and in
the plans of buildings; the clearest element in either a paint
ing or an architectural plan by Le Corbusier is the line – it

stablished a base from which he could develop ideas in
olour, light and form. But as he became more preoccupied
vith sculpture, his paintings seem increasingly to resemble
is plans for buildings; from the late 1940s until the end of
he 1950s, when they were in the process of changing again,
hey were exclusively about shapes – shapes that didn't
uite touch, but floated near each other, sometimes over-
apping. The lines behave in a similar fashion, approaching
ach other, sometimes crossing, and describing ears, breasts,
highs, heads – beautiful continuous lines making continu-
us spaces. Le Corbusier's plans possessed precisely the
ame flow of line: the exquisite details from the 1920s and
930s – the mandala forms enclosing a basin on one side, a
tair on the other, triangular cupboards, a screen spiralling
ound a bed – were no longer trapped inside a square; they
ould escape like birds into the fresh air. And so they did –
t the Ronchamp Chapel, at the Philips Pavilion at Brussels,
t the Harvard Arts Centre; and in these plans, too, was
uch the same symbolism that could be discovered in the
aintings and drawings, particularly in connection with the
ar.

The paintings explain a great deal about his buildings of
he 1950s as do his sculptures. Both had a hand in Ron-
hamp: the ear of *Josephine* and the ear symbolism of the
ainting can be seen in the plan and the listening ears of his
culpture in the light shafts. Tall and upright, they seem to
e directed across the valley, alert like the ears of a rabbit
wake to the world; but simplified so that, simultaneously
hey echo the shape of the nun, and, on yet another level,
uggest the round towers of old stone houses. Again, when
he associations have evaporated, the light shafts remain
ehind as unique – there is nothing like them anywhere.
Ior is there anything else that resembles the plan where a
ngle line connects the shafts together; these two volumes
re held in position by one unique charcoal line – and, like
he upright form, it is an abstraction of the shape of the ear.
hus, in this group, all arts seem to be in an embrace, all

assisting in the production of one piece of architectural imagery. Then another space, and a third upright form, is captured by a second line, and the third line makes the dominating wall that screens the Chapel from the south in which are set the deep windows, the scattering of coloured glass that fills the interior with spots of orange, yellow and blue.

Three lines in all, each of a different shape and curve; and three towers – could these towers be regarded partly as memorials to the three sister abbeys in the south that influenced him – in other words, to three nuns? And could they also be reminders of his passion for acoustics? Le Corbusier really did make his forms work hard – as he said, it was 'a genuine phenomenon of visual acoustics'; or as Schelling said, 'architecture was music in space, as it were frozen music...' Of the three walls which shape the building, only two short pieces are straight, the rest are curved, and there is not a single right-angle. The plan flows with the ease of a freehand drawing; yet the design is, in fact, entirely regulated by the Modulor, the dimensions of which are set out by the paving slabs on the floor.

Suddenly the inspiration for this building seems to have a very simple explanation. His penetrating gaze observed the world about him, recording anything that was, even remotely, connected with his art: this was then processed in his painting and transferred to sculpture, from which it entered his buildings. He said himself: 'It is by the channel of my painting that I came to architecture', and, since he pursued painting throughout his life, it seems likely that an important part of the inspiration for his buildings remained true to this source. And while the Modulor focussed on the importance of the proportion of the human being, the human being focussed attention on shape and free-flowing forms. The first buildings in his second twenty years fall in with this order of things: the *L'Unité*, then the Chapel. And everything which Le Corbusier had seen up to this time, all the research that he had done – and was evident in his

otes, drawings and paintings – was processed at Ron-
hamp: autobiographical, its associations arose from far
ack because he was born quite nearby. So, in a way, it
ay have been his own memorial.

There is yet another fascinating aspect to this building. In
sense, the curves, the walls which coil like shells, the risks
e took with forms were nothing new. These were all
ings which were present in the whitewashed houses he
uilt in the 1920s, at the Villas La Roche, Stein and Savoye.
n those occasions, however, the shapes were ordered by
ie outline of the cube, which was the frame. But at Ron-
namp he jettisoned the architectural frame, took it away,
aving the shapes behind, uncovered – the acoustical forms
at responded, as he suggests, only to nature, to echoes, so
at the forms became a visual diagram of rebounding
unds and sensations.

For there was a frame, after all. It was the frame of the
ur horizons that he had drawn with such meticulous care,
ch one separately, on his first visit. 'It is they who com-
anded'.

was about the time he began designing Ronchamp that he
ished his *cabinon* at Cap Martin near Monte Carlo – he
as bathing there in 1965 when he died. This was a mani-
station of the 'shack' that was so much on his mind then,
d he built it himself on Modulor dimensions: the living
ace and bedroom were planned as two squares (four
etres long and two wide), while the workroom was only
o metres square – this was all he needed. But in the same
ar (1950) he had also drawn up another, quite different
ea for a church in South America (not built and, up to
w, unpublished); it was simply a spire, or pyramid, with
equal angles. And, while Ronchamp was being built, a
ther *L'Unité* had been completed at Nantes-Rezé and
andigarh was on the way. If the *L'Unité* at Marseilles
d Nantes were, as Le Corbusier called them, temples to
e family, the Chapel was a temple to art: religion and art

often have indistinguishable characteristics: both prese
an idea which is greater than man, and man aspires to bot
Chandigarh, however, displays another dimension of I
Corbusier's genius: the ability to capture the spirit of
country and its civilization, or of a continent – its life, i
culture, its presence.

Chandigarh city centre was, of course, a tremendo
undertaking. Yet, in essence, it was merely the continuatic
of an idea Le Corbusier had been working out for years
his picture of the ordinary, human, real world which er
bodies both freedom and order, the spirit of nature and t
humanity of man. With nature on the one hand, and m
on the other, he was seeking a balance, as always, betwe
the imagination and commonsense, the discovery of whi
held the secret of true art. The inspiration for this la
period of his work lay in natural things, in natural ph
nomena – hence the emphasis laid on natural materials, fr
forms and movement. There was the invention of *bét
brut*; there were the concrete vaults that mirrored t
shapes of the snow-laden boughs of fir trees; at Ronchar
the lines of the building were as free as the lines of the hi
that surrounded the chapel. With the Modulor remaini
an active presence in the background, he could see ways
which a more indigenous style could grow from mode
architectural opportunities: he told Nehru, for instan
that Indian architecture should gather more from its ov
culture, climate and materials, and less from western ide
At Chandigarh there was no deviation from his deterr
nation to get to the heart of his picture of the ideal wor
as in a Cézanne painting, his objective was to focus on
matters that were central to this picture. He found inspi
tion in precisely the way that he had found it before –
the place as he saw it, as he found it, and in the indigenc
properties of that place. In particular, he found inspirati
from the haunches and horns of oxen.

The associations are at work again, making first imag
then their magic. 'First to look,' he said, 'and then to

serve and finally perhaps to discover.' Studies of rock forms
in nature had inspired the design for the pocket watch, and
the rippling north African coast was reflected in the vaults
of the house he designed there – he was, quite simply, a
painter. But it is very curious how the shape of this particular house returns in a drawing he did when he first arrived in India: in just the same way, the perimeter wall of
a farm building opens at the centre to reveal a glimpse of
the corrugation of roof tiles – this image occurred in the
opening in the wall of the African house. It also recalls
memories of the roof tiles at Le Thoronet, and in rural
French farm houses. This association of materials, and their
forms, brings Le Corbusier's eye for a particular shape into
sharp focus: he observed certain details which others did
not, and saw a meaning in them which passed others by.
But then, looking in Lucien Hervé's book on *Le Corbusier:
The Artist, the Writer* at this picture of the local Indian
farm building, you notice something else; it sits under a
drawing of an ox, and the shape of the wall with its open
centre reflects the form of the ox's head and horns. In the
background, behind the wall, is this corrugated roof covering a barn of some kind. Between the horns, which resemble
the sides of the high wall, Le Corbusier has drawn with the
greatest care, the ripple at the top of the ox's forehead. This
ripple is black, and the line is thick, as though he was suddenly struck with the connection between the top of the
head and the roof – the roof which shows in the picture
below. The horns were also darkly drawn, and so was the
head. Le Corbusier's comment explains the connection with
accustomed simplicity – 'to live in harmony with all men,
animals and inanimate things'. In the context of the explanation, architecture also appears very simple: a building
should describe people and a place quite as exactly as any
painting does: all man-made forms have natural origins,
and the early men who copied the outline of the cave is as
good an example as any. But on the same page of Hervé's
book there is another little sketch of great significance – a

note on a traditional cart wheel with a large wheel-brace fixed to the axle, and there are additional drawings showing the jointing of this attachment, the elevation of which was very carefully recorded. This wheel seemed to interest him because of ancient associations with the sun-wheel and other mandala forms, and he reproduced the wheel as relief sculpture on the side of a ramp. But the wheel-brace to the wheel interested him even more, perhaps, because its shape harmonized with others he had noticed, and it is possible that he noticed them because they confirmed the rightness of a picture or image that had already formed, or was forming, in his mind. For the walls of the local farm building, the horns of the oxen and the wheel-brace make shapes that rhyme with each other. If such discoveries do rhyme – as the bough of the fir rhymes with the shape of the heart and its veins, with the ear, with the leaf that also rhymes with the shape of its tree, with the shape of a bean and the breasts of a woman – the architectural forms that these rhymes suggest should have a rightness about them because they are forms that emanate from the natural evolution of things. In other words Le Corbusier was seeing visual images as a poet sees words which, when put together, make a perfect whole.

Now one begins to understand his intuition of natural phenomena; how Le Corbusier looked at the world – the imagery that was constructing itself in his mind. The shape of the horns appears in his paintings and then in the first drawings for the High Court (*see Plate 17*). The flowing lines and haunches of the animals are visible in the tremendous vaulted structure that carries the roof, and the shape of the wheel-brace reappears as the profile of the section through the roof. The theme of the horns occurs again and again – inverted in the structure of the vaults and their supports, in the principle of the sculpture of the Open Hand, in the shape of canopies, in the elevational profile of the roof at the top of the Governor's Palace; and it is vividly portrayed in the upturned portico at the entrance of the

General Assembly. It is fascinating that something so small and commonplace as horns could become an architectural theme of such an enormous size. Yet it was these forms in particular, as strongly stated against their background of hills and mountains as the ripple of the head between the horns on the original sketch, that established the correctness of Chandigarh's government buildings as part of, and inseparable from, their natural setting, and thus as a continuation of what was already present in natural things, the precise character and quality of which have been gradually evolving over thousands of years.

This discovery of the horns was similar to the discovery of the ears, and both are descriptions of Le Corbusier's sources of inspiration: observation of life, time past. He was like an echo, as he himself once suggested, of old civilizations; an eye which, like a zoom lens, holds distant objects in tight focus. It is not mere chance, for instance, that the Governor's Palace was a ziggurat, since the ziggurat was the common temple and tomb form in the Indus civilization of three to four thousand years ago. It was not mere chance that the garden in front of the Governor's Palace was to be dug out of the ground in quadrangles that made solids and voids, since this was a traditional way of building villages in the East – the houses were the solids and the entrances were the voids. In the same way, it is no coincidence that the great light shaft of the General Assembly closely resembles the shape of the traditional Indian air ventilators that are scattered across the roofs of old towns; nor that the centre of Chandigarh, and the sculpture of the Open Hand that surmounted it, was in the north-west corner, for this was the custom in grid-iron towns of the Indus. Having observed and rapidly assimilated the indigenous and traditional properties of a country and its culture, having fastened onto the essence that described the spirit of a continent – the dignity of its life and history – Le Corbusier then transforms this essence into something entirely his own. The ziggurat is seen to conform to the classical discipline of the square and the cube, and the pieces of which it is composed are then separated by *piloti*, so stressing the square form on alternate levels and recalling influences from his own work of years before – like the Villa Savoye. While, therefore, the Governor's Palace belongs both in time to the past and the present, it is also, as it must be, partly autobiographical. The sunken garden is, again, transformed into a totally original invention – the eastern village is just a spark that fires the imaginative engine. Le Corbusier turns the idea into a relief sculpture in the flat, using water, ramps, steps and vertical objects to accentuate a further dimension to the relief created by shapes shown in reflection. At the same time it is a garden, and because it is sunk, and because it is divided up into small quadrangles and other shapes with the walls of the ground to secure them, it is also shady and a shelter from the straight sun or from the wind.

A similar imaginative process can be seen at work at the General Assembly. The plan of the great light shaft describes a circle, so that the form of the shaft carries right through the interior from high above the roof to the ground. Le Corbusier then surrounds the circle with a square – offices, entrance halls and so on – and the combination of these forms carries with it the further eastern symbolism of the Circle of Heaven and the Square of man. But the circle and the square have simultaneous origins in the Greek diagram of proportion from which both the western architectural tradition and Le Corbusier stepped off. This double symbolism would have satisfied Le Corbusier's concern for unity, for the wholeness of things, particularly perhaps because Chandigarh is geographically roughly midway between the cultures of East and West. But this point leads into another. For while the enormous upturned portico which frames the involved contents of the building – all three floors of it – certainly follows the shape of the horns of the oxen, it also brings back, with a jolt, the traditional upturned eaves of the Indian and Chinese house and temple, the shape of which, if continued on its natural path, again suggests the Circle of Heaven. Here may be a clue that would account for Le Corbusier's passionate determination to get the sculpture of the Open Hand built at Chandigarh. This Hand was of enormous importance to him: he wanted it used, he would have liked people to walk about on it, so that they would become, rather like insects, aware of surroundings and details that are so small they are normally invisible to the human eye – a continuation of a theme that may be discerned at Ronchamp. But although the form of the Hand resembles the horns, or perhaps the wheel-brace, the finished work seems closer to the eastern mandala and Le Corbusier's own interpretation of that symbol in his diagram of day and night, itself a symbol, possibly, of the balance, harmony and unity he sought in his architecture (*see Plate* 20). Was the Open Hand – to give and to receive – also intended as a symbol of unity between East and West, of peace in the world, of Le Corbusier's picture of heaven?

Le Corbusier's past creeps in everywhere at Chandigarh: while he was creating new forms he was also working out other, older ideas. The interior plan of the Governor's Palace is full of curved walls, swimming about within the frame of the square like goldfish in a tank. The arrangement of spaces is as casual as the Ronchamp Chapel appears, but here it is the ziggurat, not nature, that makes the final decisions: the spaces are firmly enclosed by the sides and the 'steps' (terraces, roofs) of the form. The kind of contrast that the Jaoul house made between inside and outside is again made here at the Palace, which helps one further to understand Jaoul: the Palace façade has a strict, an almost brutal rhythm – tough enough to withstand the raw distances of landscape it overlooks, much as the ziggurat did in the Indus where it was placed in the northern corner square of the grid-iron town plan upon which Chandigarh itself was based. But, compared to the façade, the interior is entirely carefree and relaxed – as it should be in such a hot place : both are wonderfully apt analyses of function. The rhythm of the façade is then adapted for the *brise soleil* screen at the Secretariat offices. This very large building required a sun screen of a far greater complexity than the concrete louvres Le Corbusier had fitted to the glass façade at Rio, and there are traces of ideas from very early still-life paintings as this screen increases in geometric complexity towards the centre of the building. It becomes dense with verticals, horizontals and solids; a study in positives and negatives, where the solids are lit up by the bright sun and the shady glass wall behind melts away into a dark negative. The whole effect is reduced to simple lines of great vigour and formality – very different from the airiness of the Parliament building to which it is connected by a passage. Of course, it is not just a passage; it is an invention with holes – holes in blank walls of concrete, where the holes are different sorts of ovals, squares with rounded corners, all roughly circular and showing the rich colours inside. But what is a window, Le Corbusier might well be saying, if it isn't a hole? And if it is to be permanently open to keep the interior cool with breezes, let us build holes.

On one level, Le Corbusier was, through shapes derived from horns, describing the face of a place. On another level, the vast range of ideas – the sculpture of rooftops, of pyramids, cubes, cones and triangles – is unified by the simplicity with which the various structures respond to the strong sun. Framed by the blue sky, like the villages in the Greek islands, the structures appear as an assembly of sculptural objects solely shaped by light and shadow, where outlines matter far less than the voluptuous contours of forms.

But there is more to it even than this. Two enormous cool and calm reflecting lakes, each nearly three miles long, face the Himalayas in the foreground, and these produce a dual image of sky, buildings, groups of trees and mountains in the distance as beautifully composed as any painting (*see*

Plate 18). It is these flat mirrors – making it possible, Le Corbusier said, 'to see the stars in the sky and the stars in the water' at the same moment – that frame the whole centre of the city.

At the same time, these lakes solved another problem. The buildings of the city centre are not tall, yet they are seen against the huge mountains of the Himalayas which should dwarf them totally. The reflection of these buildings in the water, however, doubles their volume, while the image of the sky produces a picture of infinite depth. This simple idea provided Le Corbusier with his last aesthetic answer at Chandigarh.

4 The Dream

Quite suddenly – as suddenly as Le Corbusier dropped the cube and the concrete frame in 1930, dropped machine imagery in his paintings and then, later, dropped steel-framed structures and plain glass façades – the roughness of the late period ended. In 1968, three years after his death, the Corbusier Centre in Zurich appeared beside the lake – one final, carefree, brilliant gesture, one last blaze of fireworks (*see Plate 21*). For the Centre was made of steel and glass, it was demountable, it had a precision-made plan and surface finish, it was enamelled in the clearest collection of colours he ever used; and all the corners were square. In the middle 1950s, perhaps significantly, Le Corbusier's paintings had also changed : the flowing lines, the symbolism of the ear, the figures rolling about with the abandonment of laughter, the coloured shapes floating in a limbo of dots, had vanished, to be replaced by a geometric and much more abstract series of tapestries of far brighter colours than before, and designed to decorate various government buildings at Chandigarh. Morever, all these tapestries were square, and their subdivisions were based on combinations of the square in the Modulor measurements. And the first impression of the Corbusier Centre is of square geometry and exceedingly vivid colours; all that is left of the earlier period is a concrete ramp.

Le Corbusier had, apparently, waved a wand and had produced a fascinating little Greek temple from under his hat. It is possibly the finest thing he ever did; it has a freedom which seems greater than even Ronchamp's, and this is precisely because there is not a single curved wall or screen throughout the entire building. Here is the paradox : since the 1930s Le Corbusier had been through every free shape imaginable, and at the end of this vast research he found that what he believed was true in the first place was still true – it is the resistance of the right-angle or straight line that offers the greatest freedom. And so Le Corbusier didn't really produce the Centre from under his hat; and, in any case, the idea for it had been with him for years. As far back as 1938, it appears in an infinitely delicate and tiny ink drawing; then in 1950, this drawing reappears as the idea for a pavilion for an exhibition project in Paris – two adjoining triangulated roofs hovering over some loosely arranged things going on beneath. In 1957 the construction turns up again as part of a scheme for a museum in Tokyo – the main building was carried out, but not the pavilion. The design for it, however, been taken a little further and it was displayed as a model – two papery roofs that have, in each case, a square plan which are supported at only six points round the edges: and, once more, something rather mysterious is going on underneath these roofs. Then, at last, came the first project model for Zurich in 1963 which coincided with another experiment with the same idea for an art museum in Stockholm that would display the work of the three modern artists, Picasso, Matisse and Le Corbusier. But again, the Stockholm museum got no further than a beautiful plan for a structure floating on water. The model for Zurich, however, shows the form of the building developing fast: unlike sponsors in Paris, Tokyo and Stockholm, someone in Switzerland was clearly determined to drag the idea, so long withheld, out into the sunlight of the park beside the lake. Here, this time, was an independent roof with a concrete and glass structure beneath it. And a bubble, which had first begun to form twenty-five years before, seemed ready to burst.

The idea for this structure began to progress at a time when the *L'Unité d'habitation* at Marseilles was near completion; and it exactly coincided with the conception of the chapel at Ronchamp. The pavilion was, however, an entirely different kind of thing – precise where the spirit of the *L'Unité* was rough and heavy, geometric where the Jaoul house was voluptuous and the Chapel was abandoned, and dreamlike. Yet these were all buildings that were being designed or built when the exhibition building was first conceived. From the start the Pavilion looked different from anything else he was doing at the time, including those strange ideas for churches in South America and at Firminy in France: there was a precise geometry about the Pavilion's structure that set this design apart from the sculptural themes that had preoccupied Le Corbusier for so long at Chandigarh. And it remained separate as other ideas slowly collected round the Pavilion over the years, rather as though the design chose to lie in wait, in Le Corbusier's 'storehouse', quietly preparing for the time when the gigantic offensive of the middle and late periods that had spread itself across different continents and had reached Japan and America, had begun to exhaust itself. Then a replacement would be needed, a new point of departure.

This makes one think of something else. In the 1930s, at a time when Le Corbusier was most deeply involved with mechanization, and with a craft that had an exactness which could be compared to the best in eighteenth-century architecture, another idea of genius had cropped up in the 'weekend' house; and there was nothing sketchy about this idea. It did not have to be taken further, developed, improved upon – the house was a perfectly fulfilled design and easily as good as anything else he had done up to that time. But then the glass of the *Pavillon Suisse* and of the hostel for the Salvation Army building, for the office block in Moscow and of the flats in Geneva and Paris can, in the same kind of way, be observed evolving in the drawings of the glass towers in the green cities that he was busy planning in the early 1920s. At the same time he was, with great speed and energy, working out the whitewashed architecture of the cube at Pessac and at the Villas La Roche, Cook, Stein and Savoye. This makes an extraordinary picture of restless imaginative activity. But then the inspiration for this period was, of course, derived from the Parthenon and the project for the *Ateliers d'Artistes*, conceived when he was only twenty-three – another idea of genius which, partly because of the war, remained simmering for about ten years before it was fully enough formed to inspire his work of the 1920s. It was then that a flood of ideas – all vigorous, original and fresh – brought a new language to architecture and, in one decade, spread a white and sparkling style through Europe.

Thus a pattern emerges. As soon as a single idea of profound significance was launched, and the enormous task of developing this idea undertaken, another idea of equal significance was already forming from which he could continue when the development of the preceding idea was, at least for the time being, completed, and the energy expended on this development exhausted. Only then, only when all that could be extracted out of the idea had been taken, was he ready to begin again with the next. However, right at the source of this vast and infinitely complex story is the remarkable design for the back of the pocket watch. Within the circle of the form this design seems, in some way, to encompass the total theme of Le Corbusier's life's work. For in this microcosmic picture it is possible to perceive all the pieces – the cube, nature, harmony and balance – and to trace them through paintings, sculpture and buildings on a bewildering succession of levels. The words that Le Corbusier used to describe the magic of the abbey of Le Thoronet – the abbey which had such an impact on his work and about which he helped to make a book – could well be applied to both the watch and his own genius: 'Architecture is the unending sum of positive gestures. The whole and the details are *one*.'

And so here was this idea for a pavilion, quite sketchy at first – an idea for some kind of light roof structure protecting another indeterminate object beneath – taking root in his mind at a point when the *L'Unité d'habitation* at Marseilles was rising up towards its roof line and the drawings for the Chapel at Ronchamp had just begun. And there it remained, like a cocoon from which some day a wonderfully bright butterfly would suddenly flutter off, while a great deal was happening to Le Corbusier elsewhere. The centre of Chandigarh was in full swing. The vaults of the 'weekend' house and of Jaoul were being worked out further at Mrs Sarabhai's house at Ahmedabad, where the materials of architecture were, Le Corbusier says, 'the brick, rough concrete, white coatings, intense colours' – or just the essentials for a hot climate where least is sufficient; light and shadow, the structure overflowing with foliage, the circulation of cool breezes and the triangular shape of the tremendous concrete chute into the pool. But one feels, too, that the Pavilion was, somehow, lying in wait just below the surface of the irregular plan and umbrella roof of the Shodhan house, also at Ahmedabad, as though he was testing one or two thoughts that he was having about the Pavilion; for at Shodhan he had returned to the cube of the 1920s, and in particular to the house at Carthage where the floors themselves broke up the sun's glare with alternate balconies. The huge vertical sunbreakers of a building for an association of millowners were another experiment with light and shadow, and can be linked with the façades at the Arts Centre for Harvard. All these schemes, carried out when the Pavilion was still at conception stage, were intense, carefully woven strands of the much larger patchwork of Chandigarh where the sun, and protection from the sun, created the architectural forms; the outline, so important to him once, had retired into the shade.

His architectural drawings followed suit – the clear ink lines of plans and sections and elevations of earlier methods were also gone; at Chandigarh, at the Arts Centre, at the Shodhan house, a pen was replaced by soft pencils, and the forms were displayed with the gentlest of shading and tones. And these tones, this preoccupation with the shading, show themselves at the monastery of Sainte-Marie de la Tourette at Eveux, back in France, another building which ran paral-

lel to the buildings of Chandigarh. This was conceived in
1953 and completed in 1959, and it was a highly complex
problem: somehow the monks' cells, a chapel, dining
rooms, a library, offices and innumerable other things had
to be put together on a steep hillside with very little money
– so little that Le Corbusier accepted no fee, only his ex-
penses. Again, he was working out ideas that were governed by the movement of the sun – La Tourette is made by
light, and the control of light: if the natural laws are correctly seen and understood, the interpretation of them in
building will suit and embellish the life of man. The influence of Le Thoronet, the sister abbey of Sénanque, falls
like a shadow over La Tourette: it is present in the quadrangle, in the sharp concrete spire, in the bare simplicity of
the materials, in the stone chapel and in the circles of light
burrowing through from the ground above it. At La Tourette, the quadrangle was the frame, enclosing a collection of
sculptural objects – the spire, the triangular roofs, a cylindrical corkscrew stair, an arch, light shafts protruding
through long grass like batteries of guns – and other quadrangles; and this frame was stressed by the double floor of
monks' cells that defined the top of the building like a Renaissance frieze (*see Plate 22*). Thus the complicated features
of the monastery were brought together within a single
form that looked inwards for quiet and reflection, and outwards over the world, raised on *piloti* so that the grass of
the hillside could flow beneath, untouched.

His most important discovery at La Tourette was, perhaps, the random vertical window division that he had also
used, on occasions, at Chandigarh. He came upon this idea
partly through working with Xenakis, the composer who
was also an engineer and who, in Le Corbusier's office,
composed the sounds and electronic poetry for the Philips
Pavilion at the Brussels World Fair. Xenakis interested Le
Corbusier in the modulations of music and its subtle inflec-
tions, and Le Corbusier transferred the conception to architecture. Modulations suggest rhythms and continuity,

where windows of equal widths suggest static forms with no movement, the eye becoming focused on repeated divisions. With unequal divisions – an idea that rhymes with the diagram and theory of the Modulor – the eye can, however, wander at will, roving over a whole façade without hindrance. And so, for the first time in history, windows were allowed to have unequal widths. There was no reason why they should be equal, and architects all over the world who copied Le Corbusier's idea must have wondered why on earth they had not realized this for themselves. It was, however, Le Corbusier who invented the random window division, and his delight at this discovery shows in the flood of scattered divisions over almost the whole of La Tourette's north façade. The invention captured the random spirit of the countryside, its undulations, its freedom, its continuity and unending complexities; the divisions were like folds in curtains, and they cast long and wonderful lines of light and dark in the high rooms of the refectory and library, recalling situations at Le Thoronet where shapes are drawn by the sun in shadows on floors and walls. With, as Le Corbusier would say, a single positive gesture, La Tourette became an integral part of its indigenous setting; and the invention meant another victory over the straight line that had ruled the shape of buildings in the past. At the chapel at Ronchamp it was a sprayed cement skin on a skeleton of triangulated concrete frames clothed with a light steel mesh that had worked the magic that made the break with the straight line possible and complete. 'I like the skin of women,' Le Corbusier said, and promptly constructed a building like a person. But the random divisions gave another material its freedom: glass. A wall of glass could go, suddenly, in any direction, follow any curve without any disruption to the flow and pattern of the surface. The restrictions were finally lifted, and this is what the Arts Centre in Harvard of the early 1960s demonstrates. With the lifting of all restrictions on shape, the problem at Harvard – made excessively difficult by a narrow site (it was hardly more than a left-over gap between buildings) – appears at once quite simple, and all the limitations vanish from sight at a single stroke. What Le Corbusier did here was to collect together a number of his favourite effects and images, and these were all directed towards a common goal – a totally free shape: *piloti*, his 'dear, faithful concrete' as he called the material, the vertical louvre of immense size, the random window division and – the ear. As usual Le Corbusier was taking big risks; he was a newcomer to the scene but he would have claimed that he was only acting in the way that his forerunners in the past had done – in Venice, for instance, where, as he said in his book *Concerning Town Planning*, 'each newcomer had faith in his own adventure and, taking stock of his neighbours, risked ... dared....' A risk, all the same, requires a coherent and hard form to take charge of it, a frame. At the Arts Centre the frame is in the plan, and for the shape of this plan he returned to the image of the ear, the form that he had perfected in his paintings and sculpture, and at the Chapel at Ronchamp.

In the sculpture, for reasons of balance and tension, the ears were listening in opposite directions, and so they were at Ronchamp – two of the towers were back to back, another, the tallest, looked between them across the valley. At the Arts Centre, the ears are face to face (like the separating halves of a bean about to take root), but seen in the flat, as in the paintings, not in the upright position as in the sculpture and at Ronchamp. It is this precise juxtaposition of the two shapes – both producing slightly different abstractions of the shape of the ear, and separated by the very long, curved ramp (which, at the same time, ties them together like a knot or like the stem of the bean when it breaks in half to take root) – that makes a single statement of great power. This is the frame for the composition, and the clarity of the statement accepts all the details, the various curves, the variations of height and profile. The first phase in the architectural operation is thus established with certainty, without fear. Then the other elements enter the scene and complete the operation. The *piloti* frees the form from the ground so that it can be fully appreciated from every angle; concrete sets out the plan of the ears, and their shape. The vertical louvres, so large that they are like slanting walls which catch glancing views of the outside, and the random window divisions then describe and construct the line of the ears in three dimensions. 'The whole and its details are *one*'. Le Corbusier had completed yet another expedition 'into the inexhaustible domain of nature'.

It is, however, in this juxtaposition of the ears that one glimpses the lengthening shadow of the Corbusier Centre at Zurich, and in the visual divider of the ramp. One hears echoes; the same echoes, perhaps, which haunted the Shodhan house at Ahmedabad. Looking at Le Corbusier's work is rather like looking at the sea. Wave follows wave, wave after wave breaks on the shore. Sometimes one of the waves is taller than the rest, a white horse, pulling those that follow with greater vigour than others had before. You can see this wave from far away. It is always quite distinct and unmistakable. In 1963, when the last waves of the 1940s and 1950s brought ashore the monastery of La Tourette and the Arts building at Harvard, the Corbusier Centre – sparkling and fresh – suddenly appeared over the horizon.

Predictably, the model that was published in 1963 contained a number of Le Corbusier's favourite ideas and materials. Under the triangulated, independent roof was a building with its own roof; it had the irregular plan of the Arts Centre, but reduced down to a couple of cubes of a small size; and these cubes, separated by a ramp that shot outwards and backwards on one side, were made of concrete. One cube was largely solid, the other was an open work of random window divisions. Everything seemed poised for one final push : the grass – as spotless and smooth as a new green coat with a buttonhole of flowerbeds –

waited expectantly by the side of Zurich's calm enormous lake.

Then, in the next breath, the concrete vanished: the magician whipped away the handkerchief and there, with the exception of the ramp, was a structure of intensely bright colours made entirely of steel and glass, a construction as exquisite, sharp and accurate as the works of a watch. The idea of the design was as before. It's plan and shape was in the form of two squares, each subdivided into four spaces under the lightly supported cover, with the enclosures placed one step forward and one step back, separated by the concrete ramp. In this stunning building the influences, inventions and ideas of a lifetime – Le Corbusier's background in La Chaux-de-Fonds, his father's enamelling business, the Greek temple, derivations of the cube in the 1920s, the glass and steel of the 1930s, the roof garden, the sunshade, the Modulor and the last geometric paintings – seem to come together in a multi-coloured blaze.

The Corbusier Centre is a setting for the architecture, paintings, sculpture and writings of its maker; a place where people can meet and talk, cook a meal, have informal discussions and show the work of artists in general. An explanation for its form is given in Le Corbusier's last book, *My Work*. The whole structure is designed in terms of display: the triangulated roof is called the 'architecture', and the independent construction below is as an exhibition pavilion for the paintings and sculpture. This pavilion was, however, designed as a house, since only a house would give the right kind of domestic scale in which the paintings and sculpture should be seen; only in this way could contact be firmly established between the spectator and the object observed. And no one knows better than the general public the oppressive effects of remoteness and distant solemnity conveyed by the normal museum; it is enough to put the most hardened tourist off. 'Art,' you can hear Le Corbusier saying, 'belongs to people – to all people.'

In consequence, he designed a 'house' on two floors, and this 'house' has a kitchen, a circular stair, a ramp and a roof-terrace; ceilings, regulated by Modulor dimensions, are only 226 centimetres high – a mere seven feet six inches – and within the reach of a six foot man. There is something oddly right about a ceiling you can just about touch – it makes a special kind of relationship between the space and a person. But the low ceilings raise an exceedingly interesting point. Le Corbusier designed the 'house' to suit one set of circumstances, and irrespective of the huge size of the park. It should look absurd, impossibly small in such a situation. But here, in fact, was a perfect architectural exercise, the steps of which are set out with a mathematical exactness. Art must relate to people, and people must relate to their surroundings; but these surroundings must also relate to the outside world – the park. Hence the roof structure – the architectural frame.

This is why the roof structure is called the 'architecture': it links the exterior with the interior, the scale of the park with the scale of the 'house', which is very small – overall, it can hardly be more than fifteen feet high. But the interior has to be small to equate with a domestic scale. And inside the Centre, under a blue ceiling, you suddenly feel that you really are in a house. There is a kitchen; the addition of a bathroom and a few screens to make bedrooms – you can see where they would fit in – would complete the picture of a house. Up the blue ramp to the first floor; through some glass are the branches of trees and a glimpse of the shining lake. And then to the terrace above by the circular stair where the great structure dips down over you.

This is the climax of the building. The picture is in front of you; it is all there. You are walking about on the roof just below the red, white and green triangles, and these, pointing up and down, frame the park, making more green triangles. So you feel, from the shelter of your roof, part of the park. There seems to be no beginning and no end. Nature, and the platform under the roof, merge; from the pressed-steel seats, flowing round in a freehand line (a single memory of the free 1950s), you can sit with your back to the edge and admire the trees and the sky, under your sunshade, in your private garden. You have made the discovery that the frame and the 'house' are also really part of each other, as they are of the park. Now you begin to understand the Corbusier Centre. All the pieces of it – the spaces outside, the people and paintings, and the objects which inhabit it – are part of the same picture. As you look back across the park you see this picture by Le Corbusier as yet another double image. In one, the building suggests a temple where the frame, not unlike the portico of a Greek Megaron, shades the detail of the geometric mosaic from the glare of the sun. In the next, you discover the proportions which relate to people, and so to the spaces inside, of which the shapes outside are an exact description.

Then you notice something else. The frame assists the scaling down of the size of the park to the size of the 'house', and this process is concluded by the delicate steel structure. But, at the same time, the frame (and the dual image of it in the pool beside the pavilion) enlarge the scale of the 'house', as the porticos do at Palladio's Villa Capra – and you feel grander and more important because of this.

Still a question remains: why did Le Corbusier suddenly give up concrete and revert to the steel he used in the 1930s? For one thing, steel meant that the building could be demountable and that, if overtaken by the kind of crisis that overtook the Villa Savoye, it could be moved away. But perhaps the answer lies merely in the result; the building was much more beautiful than it would otherwise have been – concrete might have suggested an incorrect scale, and the magnificence of the coloured enamelled steel panels would have been lacking. Perhaps, again, he felt that he had, for the time being, used up the possibilities of concrete, that, like Picasso's 'green', he had finally got it out of his system and needed a change. Or perhaps, with his unfailing sense of place, it was simply that he saw that steel and glass described the sophisticated and industrialized character of Switzerland as no other materials could, just as rough concrete described the immensity of the Himalayas. Each answer must provide part of the truth, and, taken collectively, they seem adequate. But, then again, not quite; for really a much stronger force must have been at work behind the scenes than any of these conclusions suggest – the force of the continuum, the struggle to discover, and to progress. The geometry of the Corbusier Centre has to be placed beside the paintings on which Le Corbusier was then working, and the paintings have to be placed next to the plan and form (much eroded by others after Le Corbusier's death) of the hospital for Venice, to which the paintings bear such a remarkable resemblance.

All must be seen together, as though you were in the artist's studio and he was laying out his works against the wall as he did on the pages of his books. The bough of the fir and the veins of the heart have to be put with the vaults of Jaoul and Sarabhai, and close to the ear of the sculpture which should be near the light shafts of Ronchamp, but before the horns of the oxen which should be beside Chandigarh. A circular diagram of the mandala should be put next to his drawing of the movements of the sun (*see Plate 20*), and this has to be put beside the Open Hand to which it led, and also next to the triangulated roofs of the Corbusier Centre – one pointing up, one pointing down – which it must also have inspired. Was this building the beginning of a new phase? If so, where would *it* have led?

Le Corbusier's work seems to fall into two distinct parts: what he accomplished before the Second World War, and what he accomplished after it. In the first it was the imagination of the mind that was, perhaps, the controlling influence; in the second, his medium mastered, the imagination of the senses seems to emerge as the stronger force. Finally, it is the work he did in these last twenty years that is the real memorial to his patience, dedication, modesty and faith. But in the Corbusier Centre, and in the outstretched form of the Venice hospital, sleeping its way across canals and inlets, the two great influences in his life appear to merge: perhaps this was the dream.

Yet the rhythm of ideas, and the development of these ideas, which occurred with great regularity from the moment the idea for the pocket watch was born to the building of the Corbusier Centre, indicate a possibility which may have been, in Le Corbusier's eyes at any rate, the frame for the whole of his work. The idea for a new phase took time to form – ten years or more. Far in the background, lingering on the horizon while innumerable other waves broke on the shore, was a much larger wave, and only the reverberations and side-effects generated by its force ever touched land. Le Corbusier's plans for cities never got further than the *Unités*, Chandigarh and projects. According to the natural evolution of things, architecture had to come first because it had to be understood first; to design cities without the understanding, knowledge and experience of architecture would be, as he said when he was in his early twenties, like 'wanting to sing when one does not yet have the lungs'. Nevertheless, in his book *Concerning Town Planning*, published in 1946, and quite as important as its predecessor, *Towards a New Architecture*, published twenty years before, he sets out the town planner's aims – what these were in the past, and how they should be understood, continued and developed in the twentieth century.

His argument is very simple. In his diagram of a meandering village street he shows the situation before the cart: it was possible to have these meandering streets in which people walked, and he loved them. But as populations increase, and knowledge advances and the scale becomes altogether bigger, it becomes necessary, in order to keep the human jumble intact, and to preserve the humanity and character of the jumble, to make a bigger, more positive gesture – the kind of gesture, vast and explicit, with which whitewash contains the jumble of Greek island architecture against a blue sky. The Place des Vosgues, the square built in Paris in 1606, was just such a gesture. He writes: '... in the tall tangle of Gothic Paris, crammed within its walls: the Place des Vosgues, tailored from one piece, an act of will, of royal will: the master ordains.' What he means is that a frame was required to give an order to the communities within it and which centred round such important people as the grocer, the butcher, and the postman, who, in their smaller way, made their own frame for the community as represented by the meandering street. The Piazza Navona is another positive gesture; and so is the Capitol in Rome, based on Carlsruhe, of which Le Corbusier draws an aerial plan. The 'act of will, of royal will' that 'the master ordains' is imposed on the overlapping, intersecting circles of the communities governed by the grocer and the postman by a force outside these communities, the force that made the Place des Vosgues, and the Capitol.

But in the twentieth century a bigger gesture was required because, again, the problems were bigger, if the humanity – the intersecting circles of the various communities – of cities was to remain intact. And so, in 1922, Le Corbusier made his first positive gesture in his city for three million inhabitants. From the beginning he saw the problems surrounding the car unfolding, and from the beginning, too, he was emphatic that pedestrians and cars must be separated; cars and their drivers prefer straight lines, so they should be situated overhead, and people, who like terra firma and wandering, might remain on the ground, in 'the green perspectives of the park'. Tall towers were designed so that parks could be made, sunlight and air could be enjoyed, flats could look down on an eiderdown of foliage through which the glass forms arose. He never intended that there should be an epidemic of concrete towers any more than he intended that these towers should be surrounded with black asphalt, paving and car parks. This is not what he meant at all. Once again, however, his imitators copied his outlines and ignored the underlying

principles from which these outlines evolved. In consequence disastrous damage has been done throughout the
world.

The positive gesture in planning was always, as with his
buildings, as with the Place des Vosgues, founded on a
frame, and within this frame, as his buildings, there was
order, space, easy communications, air, sunlight, grass and
trees. These were the principles that governed the design and
which had, at all costs, to be maintained. Le Corbusier
knew exactly what he was doing as a town planner because
he knew what lines meant when he drew them : he saw
real people in the real surroundings of real buildings : the
grass was real and so were trees : nothing was an abstraction. But first there was the frame, the positive gesture of
great size. That this was the first priority is clear from the
remarkable conceptions for Rio and Buenos Aires in 1929,
and for São Paulo of the same year. At Rio there was the
sea and the irregular coastline of mountains and hills. In
precisely the way that he conceived an idea for a building
by taking stock of the neighbours and surroundings, Le
Corbusier took stock of Rio's whole panoramic view. His
conception for the city thus became the combined effort of
the mountainous profile and one immensely long building
three hundred feet high that wound its way between the
lower mountains and carried the main highway above it,
putting off cars at convenient hill-tops. The simplicity of
the idea is as childlike as it is practical and sensational. The
scheme for São Paulo made a similar gesture, but there the
city was constructed of two very long buildings in the form
of a cross. And in 1934 he designed the new city for Algiers.
This plan sets out more plainly, perhaps, than any other,
the aims for which he argues in *Concerning Town Planning*
(*see Plate 11*).

In this city, his ideas had changed. As in his paintings, he
had dropped straight lines and right-angles and had gone
over to curves : and as in his paintings too, he seemed to be
using the town plan for experiments with shapes. And so it

becomes clear that his planning was as necessary to his architecture as his painting and sculpture were both necessary to his architecture and to his planning. As with the park and the roof garden at the Corbusier Centre, there is no beginning and no end; each conception belonged in part to another, in the same way that the parts of which the conception was itself composed were inseparable. When you draw away from Le Corbusier's work, what you see is relationships; and, at Algiers, what you see is a clear relationship between all his arts – planning, painting, sculpture and architecture. For here he was thinking in the widest possible terms, his imagination was able to open up on the largest possible scale, and his lines could really flow. In the first place the plan demonstrates that the positive gesture can preserve the character of the old city, and this is made with an immensely long coastline building which defines the edge of the sea and gives order to the hills, as at Rio; then, this 'sea-wall' separates the old town from the new town, thus protecting the old from a conflict with the new and keeping the character of human muddle as well. But at the same time you notice that the 'sea-wall' makes the shape of an ear, and that the complex arrangement of forms that create the new town at one end suggests the lobe of the ear which the intricate, crooked streets of the old town then adorn like an ornament. So Algiers, you discover, introduced the form of the ear to his architecture long before its manifestations in painting and sculpture were communicated to a building. And then, a moment later, you notice something quite startling. The new town, a gesture of great vigour in itself, is made from the shapes of various curved buildings that again follow the form of ears – like question marks, the ears are listening in different directions, as though to the sound of the sea. These shapes, which never touch at any point, protect an interior space – the kind of space that you find at the Villa Stein, but with the frame of the classical sides removed. And so you discover, as you look down at the plan of Algiers, that you are really looking down at something which is very like the plan for the Chapel at Ronchamp.

None of Le Corbusier's cities were built; they got no further than drawings and models. And at Chandigarh, where he designed only the government buildings, he could do no more than set out a plan that would establish the city's position in the vast plain under the Himalayas – hence the compact grid-iron. Once more he was following the traditional pattern of the builders of the ancient Indus civilization, and this form was sufficiently coherent to order the contribution of other architects. But he was most disappointed with the results, and it was then that he told Nehru that India should take inspiration from her own cultures, and not from those of the West. He became, as time went on, totally disillusioned: his *Unité* at Nantes-Resé, Meaux, Briey-en-Forêt and Berlin were eroded by shortage of money, their essential variations taken from them, and they lost the life and freshness that Marseilles possessed; the *L'Unité* at Berlin was not even built according to his drawings. A month or two before he died four city plans were turned down, and it is not surprising that he said to the English journalist who was in his office the very morning this happened: 'I see no hope.'

Le Corbusier would not have wanted us to copy him, in the same way that he did not copy the ancient Greeks – we would do better to see him as he saw the Greeks: as an age. After all, he created modern architecture. He tried everything, invented structures, explored all possible forms and materials – it seems inconceivable that any architect in the future could discover more. He had seen, within the space of his lifetime, his ideas catch fire and spread across Europe and the world, and he had seen the destruction of a dream as values and taste collapsed in the face of the materialism that followed the Second World War. Yet despite all this, despite the constant disappointments, he never gave up.

Perhaps it was in the same week that he said that he saw no hope that he wrote out the last statement of his aims and faith: 'J'ai 77 ans et ma morale peut se résumer à ceci: dans le vie il faut faire. C'est-à-dire agir dans la modestie, l'exactitude, la précision. La seule atmosphere pour une création artistique c'est la regularité, la modestie, la continuité, la persévérance. . . .'

But there was no more time: he had climbed his last mountain. It is somehow poetic that Le Corbusier should have died swimming in the Mediterranean, suddenly, and under a blue sky.

Chronology

1887	6 October, Charles-Edouard Jeanneret, the future Le Corbusier, born at La Chaux-de-Fonds, Jura, Switzerland. His father was an engraver of watch-cases and and his mother a musician.
1900	Enrolled in École d'Art of La Chaux-de-Fonds to serve his apprenticeship as engraver and chiseller. Under Charles L'Eplattenier he studied from nature and had his first instruction in the history of art.
1902	Awarded the Diploma of Honour at the International Exhibition of the Decorative Arts in Turin for an engraved watch design.
1905	Built his first house at La Chaux-de-Fonds for his teacher, L'Eplattenier.
1906	On the advice of L'Eplattenier, who was encouraging him to take up architecture, he visited Italy: Florence, Siena and Pisa.
1907	Visited Vienna and there frequented Josef Hoffmann's studio, and also became acquainted with the ideas of Adolf Loos.
1908	Went to Paris and was employed in Auguste Perret's studio where he learnt the importance of building in reinforced concrete, and studied architectural development.
1910	Retired with his text books to the mountains at La Chaux-de-Fonds to study the calculations of reinforced concrete. Later went to Peter Behrens' studio in Berlin where he met Mies van der Rohe and Walter Gropius.
1911–12	Travelled to the Balkans, Greece and Asia Minor on a study tour. He made an important series of drawings and designs.
1913	On his return to Europe he came into contact with various elements of the *avant-garde*. The elements

	of his architecture which he outlined at this time can be seen clearly in the design for the *Dom-ino* house.
1914	Returned to La Chaux-de-Fonds to teach architecture in a new section of the Art School.
1917	He returned to Paris to live, and became a friend of the painter Amédée Ozenfant. His first experiments in painting date from this time.
1918	In collaboration with Ozenfant published the manifesto *Après le Cubisme*, signalling the foundation of the Purist movement.
1920	With Ozenfant and the poet Paul Dermée formed an international review of aesthetics, *L'Esprit Nouveau*. He adopted the pseudonym 'Le Corbusier'. Also at this time he worked on the Citrohan house and launched the idea of the *machine à habiter*.
1921	With his cousin, Pierre Jeanneret, opened a studio at 35, rue de Sèvres, where he was to work until 1965.
1922	Plan for 'a contemporary city for three million inhabitants' constructed – to be exhibited at the Paris *Salon d'Automne*. Designed and built a studio house for Ozenfant and a villa at Vaucresson.
1923	Publication in *L'Ésprit Nouveau* of a series of articles which make up the substantial part of *Vers une Architecture*.
	Project for the Roche-Jeanneret house in Paris dates from this period, as does the plan for the *immeubles-villas* projects.
1925	For the International Exhibition of Decorative Arts in Paris he designed the pavilion of *L'Ésprit Nouveau*, which was a prototype of one of the living cells of the *immeubles-villas*, and in it exhibited his *Plan Voisin* for Paris.
	He built a little house on Lake Geneva near Vevey for his parents, and, using ideas from the Citrohan house scheme, planned and built a housing estate at Pessac near Bordeaux.
1926	Several buildings completed: a studio for an artist at Boulogne-sur-Seine, the *Palais du Peuple* for the Salvation Army in Paris, the *Fondation de Polignac*

building, Paris, the Maison Cook at Boulogne-sur-Seine, and the Maison Guiette at Antwerp.

1927   An important year which saw the building – following the strict rules of the *tracés regulateurs* – of the Villa Stein at Garches, and the study for the project submitted to the competition for the Palace of the League of Nations in Geneva.

Planned and built two buildings for the experimental *Weissenhof* quarter in Stuttgart.

1928   With Siegried Giedion and other leading architects of the modern movement, he founded the CIAM (*Congrès International d'Architecture Moderne*) which had its first Congress at La Sarraz in Switzerland. Its aim was to defend the cause of modern architecture.

The Villa Savoye was designed in this year and completed in 1930, at Poissy near Paris. Also, some furniture designs were drawn up, the most famous being the *chaise-longue* and the armchairs: they were not to go into mass-production till 1965.

Plans were started for the commission from the Government of the U.S.S.R. for the Palace of the Union of the Co-operatives in Moscow. The Restaurant at Ville d'Avray and the Nestlé pavilion were completed.

1929   During a lecture tour in South America he studied the problem of the expansion of the cities of Rio de Janeiro, São Paulo, Montevideo and Buenos Aires, and drafted town-planning schemes for them.

1930   Drafted a plan for the rebuilding of the city of Algiers, and for the *Pavillon Suisse* in the *cité universitaire* in Paris.

In December he married Yvonne Gallis, an attractive fashion model born in Monaco with whom he had been living for several years. She died in 1957.

1931   The major project of the competition for the Palace of the Soviets in Moscow was given much study, but again the submission was rejected in favour of a design by a Russian architect.

Plans for a 'growing' Museum of Contemporary Art were initiated.

The Salvation Army hostel in Paris was designed and

	built, incorporating the first glass curtain wall to be hermetically sealed.
1932	The building of the Clarté block in Geneva which had the first duplex apartment.
1933	Study for an apartment building in Algeria using *brise-soleil* was in hand, as was the project for *la ville radieuse* (to be published in 1938) and the town-planning scheme for Nemours in Algeria.
1935	Visited the U.S.A. to give a series of lectures, and started the controversy on the New York skyscrapers which he took up on his return to Europe in the book *Quand les cathédrales étaient blanches. Voyages au pays des timides.*
	Built a small holiday house on the outskirts of Paris and another at Mathés.
1936	Invited to be an adviser on the council for the project for the new Ministry of Education and Public Health in Rio de Janeiro.
	He was also working on town-planning schemes to improve Paris.
1937	For the International Exhibition in Paris he erected the *Pavilion des Temps Nouveaux.*
1938	Project for the Cartesian skyscraper and the plan for Buenos Aires.
1939–45	He published *La Charte d'Athènes* with an introduction by Jean Giraudoux, and *Les Trois Etablissements Humains.*
	He also continued his work on the projects for the plan of Algiers.
1945	Resumed his studies of *tracés regulateurs*, and proposed the Modulor design.
	Continued with his plans for the reconstruction of Saint-Dié, which, though never realised, were the prototype for *L'Unité d'Habitation* at Marseilles.
1947	As a member of the International Commission formed to study the project for the headquarters of the UN, he put forward the basic ideas for the realisation of the complex but was dismissed before it was built.
	Designed a housing complex for Cap Martin (and built himself a small house there); designed the

CIAM grid; an underground church for Saint-Baume; city plans for La Rochelle and Bogotà. Began to work on the Chapel of Notre Dame du Haut at Ronchamp, completed in 1954.

1951   From this year he was chiefly occupied with the preparation of plans and projects for Chandigarh, the great Punjab capital.

1952–60   Saw the building of *L'Unité d'Habitation* at Nantes and another in Berlin; the Philips pavilion at the Brussells World Fair; a museum; villas; the building for the Weavers Association at Ahmedabad in India; a museum in Tokyo; and the Dominican monastery of La Tourette at Eveux, Lyons.

1961–65   He designed the French embassy in Brasilia; a Congress Hall in Strasbourg; an Electronic Calculation Centre for Olivetti at Rho-Milan; a youth centre at Firminy; an exhibition pavilion at Zurich; and the Visual Arts Centre at Cambridge, Massachusetts, USA.

1965   27 August, Le Corbusier died of a heart attack while swimming in the sea off Cap Martin.

Short Bibliography

SOME BOOKS BY LE CORBUSIER

Après le Cubisme Jwith A. Ozenfant) (Paris: Commentaires, 1918)

Vers une architecture (Paris: Crès, 1923; English translation by F. Etchells, *Towards a New Architecture*, London: John Rodker, 1927)

Urbanisme (Paris: Crès, 1925; English translation by F. Etchells, *The City of Tomorrow and its Planning*, London: Architectural Press, 1929)

Précisions sur un état présent de l'Architecture et de l'Urbanisme (Paris: Crès, 1930)

Quand les cathédrales etaient blanches, Voyages aux pays des timides (Paris: Plon, 1937; English translation by F. E Hyslop, *When the Cathedrals were White*, London: Routledge & Kegan Paul, 1948)

La Ville radieuse (Paris, 1938; translated as *The Radiant City* London: Faber & Faber, 1967)

Sur les 4 Routes (Paris, 1941; English translation by Dorothy Todd, *The Four Routes*, London: Dennis Dobson, 1948)

La Charte d'Athènes (With a preface by J. Giradoux, repr. Paris 1957) (Paris: Plon, 1943)

Propos d'Urbanisme (Paris: Bourrelier, 1946; English translation by C. Entwhistle, *Concerning Town Planning*, London: Architectural Press, 1947)

Le Modulor (Boulogne-sur-Seine, 1949; English translation by P. de Francia and A. Bostock, *The Modulor*, London: Faber & Faber, 1954)

Poésie sur Alger (Paris: Falaise, 1950)

L'Unité d'habitation de Marseille (Mulhouse: Point, 1950; English translation by G. Sainsbury, *The Marseilles Block*, London: Harvill Press, 1953)

Une petite Maison (Zürich: Girsberger, 1954)

Le Modulor II (Boulogne-sur-Seine, 1955; *English translation* by P. de Francia and A. Bostock, London: Faber & Faber, 1958)

Le Poème de l'angle droit (Paris: Verve, 1955)

Les Plans Le Corbusier pour Paris 1922–56 (Paris: Editions de Minuit, 1956)

Ronchamp (Zürich: Girsberger, 1955; English translation by J. Cullen, *The Chapel at Ronchamp*, London: Architectural Press, 1957)

Mon Oeuvre (Paris, 1960; English translation by James Palmes, *My Work*, London: Architectural Press, 1960)

Oeuvre Complète, ed. W. Boesiger *et al*. Volume I, 1910–1929; Volume II, 1929–1934; Volume III, 1934–1938; Volume IV, 1938–1946; Volume V, 1946–1952; Volume VI, 1952–1957; Volume VII, 1957–1965 (First six volumes, Zürich: Girsberger; seventh volume, Zürich: Les Editions d'Architecture; English translation by J. Palmes, *The Complete Architectural Works of Le Corbusier*, including Volume VIII, *Les dernières oeuvres*, London: Thames & Hudson, 1970)

SOME BOOKS ABOUT LE CORBUSIER

Blake, P. *Le Corbusier* (Harmondsworth: Penguin, 1963)

Boesiger, W. & Girsberger, H. *Le Corbusier* (London: Thames & Hudson, 1967)

Damaz, Paul *Art in European Architecture* (London: Chapman & Hall, 1956)

Evenson, Norma *Chandigarh* (London: Cambridge University Press, 1966)

Gauthier, M. *Le Corbusier ou l'architecture au service de l'homme* (Paris: Denöel, 1944)

Heppenstall, R. & Cali, F. *Architecture of Truth* (London: Thames & Hudson, 1957)

Hervé, Lucien *Le Corbusier: The artist, the writer* (London: Thames & Hudson, 1957)

Jordan, R. F. *Le Corbusier* (London: Dent, 1972)

Mumford, Lewis *The Culture of Cities* (London: Secker, 1938)

Petit, Jean *Le Corbusier Lui-Même* (Geneva, 1970)

Richards, J. M. *An Introduction to Modern Architecture* (Harmondsworth: Penguin, 1940; 3rd edition, 1957)